Reviews and Comments on the First Edition

"Penetrating analysis . . . crisp and simple language . . . as revealing as it is succinct . . . an effective antidote to the mood of resignation before the omnipotence of transnational business institutions which pervades the political discourse of our times . . . timely and important."
—David Montgomery, *The Nation*

"Brecher and Costello offer compelling evidence that economic globalization largely benefits the affluent and harms the less affluent. The authors provide substantial documentation for their position. The book is well written without academic jargon, making it readable for anyone with a serious interest in political or economic affairs."
—*Choice*

"An extremely accessible account of the process of 'globalization' . . . a practical guide to what people can do about it."
—*The Ecologist*

"Popular in style . . . packed with memorable titles [and] subtitles . . . offers a thought-provoking and easily-read alternative. In the face of economic reductionism and market fundamentalism, this suggests not only a political but an ethical agenda."
—*Development and Change*

"This book is much more than a critique of the new economic world order. It's a practical guide for action for those who want to think globally and work locally on the economy, trade, and the environment."
—Elaine Bernard, director, Harvard University Trade Union Program

"Brecher and Costello's critique of the current drift of the world economy is devastating, but the greatest value of their book is to depict an emerging politics of grassroots resistance that creatively opens up a new range of radical possibilities for the 1990s."
—Richard Falk, professor of International Law, Princeton University

"It is only with the brave thinking and strategies put forth by Brecher and Costello in this hopeful book that humans of diverse concerns and interests can pursue a course for collective economic development more life-sustaining to the Earth we inhabit."
—M. Annette Jaimes, editor, *The State of Native America*

"Finally someone has stopped long enough to document with real insight and clear analysis the exciting new developments in people-to-people global networking. Brecher and Costello have a lifetime of experience that shows in their writing and their prescriptions. They're strong lights on the pathway."
—Mark Ritchie, director, Institute for Agriculture and Trade Policy

"An important, uniquely comprehensive blending of practical and visionary discussion on how to create a viable world community in a time in which corporations increasingly have power to dictate policies that increase conflict and lower standards of living around the world."
—John Brown Childs, professor, Sociology, University of California at Santa Cruz, Chair, Race and Ethnicity Research Council

"Brecher and Costello introduce us to local women's groups, from Chiapas to Arkansas to Manila, that are analyzing this not-so-new World Order most revealingly, and in doing so make us smarter."
—Cynthia Enloe, author, *The Morning After: Sexual Politics at the End of the Cold War*

Global Village
or
Global Pillage

Second edition

Jeremy Brecher
Tim Costello

Global Village
or Global Pillage

Economic Reconstruction
from the Bottom Up

Second edition

**By
Jeremy Brecher
and
Tim Costello**

**South End Press
Cambridge, Massachusetts**

Cover by Sadie Jernigan
Page design and production by the South End Press collective
Printed in the U.S.A.

Library of Congress Cataloging-in-Publication Data

Brecher, Jeremy.
Global village or global pillage : economic reconstruction from the bottom up/ by Jeremy Brecher and Tim Costello. — 2nd ed.
    p. cm.
Includes bibliographic references and index.
ISBN 0-89608-592-9. — ISBN 0-89608-591-0 (pbk.)
    1. Economic history—1990- 2. Income distribution. 3. Distributive justice. 4. Economic policy. 5. International economic relations.
I. Costello, Tim.   II. Title.
    HC59.15.B74   1998
    338.9—dc21   98-22232
                                        CIP

South End Press, 7 Brookline Street, #1, Cambridge, MA 02139-4146

04 03 02 01 00 99   2 3 4 5 6 7

Union printed

This book is dedicated to Claire Costello,
Susanne Rasmussen, and Jill, Fanya, and Moira Cutler

Contents

Acknowledgements

We thank the International Labor Rights Research and Education Fund for graciously tolerating the title of this book, notwithstanding its similarity to the title of our pamphlet *Global Village vs. Global Pillage: A One-World Strategy for Labor* published by them. We thank *The Nation*, *Z*, and *Z Papers* for permission to use material in this book that originally appeared in their magazines.

We are extremely grateful to those who read and commented on part or all of drafts of the manuscript: Elaine Bernard, Martin Bresnick, John Cavanagh, John Brown Childs, Lance Compa, Karen Crosby, Jill Cutler, Peter Dorman, Fred Glass, Ruth Glasser, Pharis Harvey, Allen Hunter, David Korten, Paul Kumar, Peter Marris, Michael Pertschuk, Mark Ritchie, Primitivo Rodriguez, and our editor at South End Press, Sonia Shah.

We would also like to thank those who provided information or helped in other ways, including Patricia Bauman, Ron Blackwell, Cam Duncan, Ed Feigen, Ken Galdston, Karen Hansen-Kuhn, Thea Lee, David Ranney, Saskia Sassen, Barbara Shailor, Bruce Shapiro, Joe Uehlein, Nikos Valance, Stephen Veiderman, Peter Waterman, and Matt Witt.

Finally, thanks to Richard Falk for suggesting that this book be written.

Introduction to the Second Edition

This book has a simple argument:

- Capital can move around the world with less and less regard for national boundaries.
- The result is a global "race to the bottom" in which workers, communities, and whole countries are forced to compete by lowering wages, working conditions, environmental protections, and social spending.
- The downward pressures of the race to the bottom are stimulating resistance all over the world.
- This competitive pressure is also creating "globalization from below"—a common interest in resisting the race to the bottom, which is reflected in developing alliances among workers, farmers, environmentalists, consumers, poor people, and people of conscience that cross national borders and the global division of North and South.

How does this argument fit the facts today?

Footloose Capital

Today, more than $1.5 trillion flows daily across international borders,[1] up by one-third in the four years since this book was written. Private financial flows to developing countries grew from $44 billion in 1990 to $161 billion in 1994 and $256 billion in 1997.[2] Direct investment abroad by "American" companies has grown so rapidly that the value of the goods and services they produce and sell outside the United States is now three times the total value of all American exports.[3]

International institutions have expanded their ability to block anything democratic governments might do to "interfere" with the mobility of private capital. The World Trade Organization (WTO) ruled against significant parts of the U.S. Clean Air Act and against U.S. laws protecting sea turtles. Legislators in Massachusetts were told that if they tried to boycott products made in Burma to protest human rights violation, there, the United States would be subject to WTO sanctions. Meanwhile, many European countries have adopted a common currency and negotiations have been launched for a free trade zone to cover the entire Western Hemisphere.

In addition to more downsizing and international outsourcing, corporations such as Chrysler and Daimler-Benz have begun merging across national lines on an unprecedented scale. Former U.S. trade representative Mickey Kantor said that troubles of the Asian "tiger" economies should be seized as golden opportunities for the West to reassert its commercial interests[4]; and indeed, U.S. companies have been buying up Asian companies at "fire sale" prices.

Race to the Bottom

The "race to the bottom" is now threatening to become a "free-fall to the bottom."

Irwin Gordon, head of the Ava-Line lapel pin manufacturer in Whippany, New Jersey, explained his company's success to *Business Week*:

> We have a factory in China where we have 250 people. We own them; it's our factory.... We pay them $40 a month and they work 28 days a month.... [T]hey work from 7 a.m. to 11 p.m. with two breaks for lunch and dinner. ... They eat all together, 16 people to a room, stacked on four bunks to a corner.... Generally, they're young girls that come from the hills.[5]

Even countries like Haiti and Bangladesh find their conditions driven downward by such competition. A subcontractor in Haiti, where the prevailing wage is 28 cents an hour, announced plans in 1997 to move to China and Indonesia, where they expected to pay 13 cents an hour.[6]

Bangladeshi trade union leader Nazrul Islam Khan described how international competition forces his country to maintain child labor:

> We want to eliminate the circumstances which are forcing those young children to work. Then the Western countries advise us to accept a free market economy. It is they that prescribe structural adjustment policies. It is they who force us into competition in the world market. It is the industrialists of these countries that are going to

China. Communism is there. Liberties are not there. Prison labor is being deployed to work. They are going to Vietnam where still one party rule is there. Now Bangladesh will have to be in competition with these countries. It is very difficult.[7]

The triumph of "free-market" capitalism was represented by Mexico, East Asia, and Russia. Now all are in economic shambles. The wages of Mexican manufacturing workers fell from 22 percent of those in the United States in 1980 to 8 percent in 1996.[8] In two years, Malaysia's economy shrunk by 25 percent, South Korea's by 45 percent, and Thailand's by 50 percent. Indonesia's economy shrunk by 80 percent; its per capita gross domestic product dropped from $3,500 to less than $750; and 100 million people, nearly half the population, sank below the poverty level.[9] In Russia, real income has fallen 40 percent since the Soviet Union collapsed in 1991[10]; the life expectancy for men has declined by seven years, to 59.[11]

These have been touted as "boom" years in the United States; but, in fact, the incomes of working people here have also been driven down in the "global hiring hall." The gross domestic product of the United States has grown more than 40 percent in the past quarter century, while the real median income of more than 60 percent of American workers has fallen.[12] The paltry wage increases of the past year have not even brought most workers back to where they were before the last recession,[13] let alone made a significant dent in the losses of the past 25 years. Average hourly wages were $9 per hour in 1973; after the increases of 1997, they were $1 an hour lower, adjusted for inflation.[14]

Household debt reached 91 percent of disposable personal income in 1997, compared with 65 percent in 1980.[15] A study based on interviews with 28,000 people in soup kitchens, homeless shelters, and food pantries found that 26 million Americans visited charitable food programs in 1997—a 15 percent increase over the year before.[16] Meanwhile, CEO salaries grew to 326 times that of the average factory worker.[17] Bill Gates owns more wealth than America's 100 million poorest people.[18]

The global economy has moved into a new phase of chronic crisis.[19] Paul Krugman, professor of economics at the Massachusetts Institute of Technology, observes, "We are back to a volatile, predepression world economy of financial booms and busts."[20]

All over the world, people are finding themselves reduced from human beings with the right to speak, vote, organize, and act collectively—and entitled to food, housing, healthcare, and job security—to mere flotsam and jetsam of the labor market, surviving only by selling their labor on a short-term, contingent basis. Meanwhile, their environment is being destroyed by an unrestrained global economy that poisons the air and water, turns plains into deserts, chops down the forests, and disturbs the most basic balance on which all life depends through the uncontrolled emission of greenhouse gasses.

Revolts and Resistance

According to labor journalist Kim Moody, "In the last couple of years there have been at least two dozen political general strikes in Europe, Latin America, Asia, and North America. This phenomenon began in 1994. There have been more political mass strikes in the last two or three years than at any time in the 20th century."[21] Since 1996, there have been general strikes in Argentina, Belgium, Brazil, Canada, Columbia, Denmark, Ecuador, France, Greece, Haiti, Italy, Puerto Rico, South Korea, and Spain, among others.[22]

For example, in France, when the government proposed to cut back pensions for transportation workers and civil servants to increase the nation's "competitiveness," a general strike and mass demonstrations disrupted the entire life of the country, forcing the government to withdraw the plan. In Korea, at the end of 1996, the ruling party passed new laws restricting workers' rights. South Korea's president said the new laws would "provide significant impetus for improved competitiveness." More than 400,000 workers joined a general strike and organized massive demonstrations; after several weeks, the government backed down and withdrew the new labor laws.

In response to the Asian financial crisis and the International Monetary Fund (IMF) "rescue" of Asian economies in 1998, mass demonstrations by students and the poor brought down the Suharto dictatorship in Indonesia. Tens of thousands of workers in South Korea struck not just against their own employers but against the policies imposed by the IMF.

Late in 1997, Democratic President Bill Clinton and his arch-rival Republican Speaker of the House Newt Gingrich cooperated to support a law known as "fast track," which would allow the president to negotiate new trade agreements without Congressional amendment. The law was strongly supported by the corporate community. Opponents stressed that the agreements authorized under "fast track" would not protect either workers or the environment. A *Business Week* poll released in September 1997 revealed that 87 percent of Americans believed that environmental protections should be advanced in trade agreements and 73 percent believed that labor rights should be included. A coalition that included labor, environmental, farm, and many other groups successfully blocked the passage of "fast track"—the first major check to the growing power of global trade organizations.

Meanwhile, an anti-sweatshop campaign has drawn millions of people into struggles around conditions in the global factory. It forced Nike to state that it would limit child labor and open its factories throughout the world to inspection by independent monitors. International manufacturers similarly agreed to limit child labor in the making of soccer balls. The city of North Olmsted, Ohio, even passed an ordinance requiring suppliers to the city to certify that their goods are not manufactured in sweatshops. San Francisco and other cities soon followed suit.

Globalization from Below

The new forms of transnational cooperation among popular social movements that have developed since 1994 could fill an entire book. Here are just a few examples:

When the governments of the Western Hemisphere launched their plans for a Free Trade Area of the Americas, trade unions, environmentalists, human rights organizations, and other non-governmental organizations launched the idea of a Hemispheric Social Alliance. They met in Santiago, Chile, in April 1998, just ahead of the Heads of State Summit there, and developed a proposal for "Social and Economic Alternatives to the Free Trade Area of the Americas." It proposed "a set of fundamental principles and ideas which could underlie an alternative to the current form of globalization, which is dominated and driven by multinational corporations and where integration equals subordination."[23]

In 1997, 200,000 UPS employees struck against the growth of part-time employment, the largest strike in the United States in 20 years. The Teamsters union and the International Transport Workers Federation organized a UPS World Council and a UPS World Action Day, with 150 job actions and demonstrations at UPS facilities worldwide. British UPS workers organized a support sickout—dubbed the "Brown Flu." Belgian workers held a wildcat strike, and unions in France, Holland, and Germany voted to call a European-wide strike action. In India, railroad workers refused to transport UPS packages; in the Philippines, a 100-car motorcade surrounded UPS's subcontractor and prevented deliveries for a day. A study of the strike concludes that some of those directly involved in the negotiations felt that international actions "were an important factor that precipitated the UPS settlement."[24]

A worldwide campaign with demonstrations in Japan, work stoppages and slowdowns in Brazil and Argentina, and bargaining demands in Belgium, France, Italy, and Spain pressured the Bridgestone/Firestone company to rehire some 2,300 U.S. workers they had discharged and replaced.[25]

At a rank-and-file level, there has been a considerable growth of local-to-local contacts among workers in the same industries, for example through tours and "sister local" affiliations, especially with Mexico and Central America. In November 1997, the San Francisco Labor Council and the California Labor Federation brought together 400 trade union and community delegates from 20 countries for the Western Hemisphere Workers' Conference Against NAFTA and Privatizations.

A 1998 global march against child labor was kicked off in Thailand with delegations from the Philippines, Bangladesh, and Indonesia.[26] The march took place on five continents, with the aim to establish a worldwide movement to promote the rights of all children to receive an education and to be free from exploitative work.

And in May 1998, 50,000 people in Birmingham, England, formed a human chain around the leaders of the G-7, the world's seven richest nations, to urge them to reduce the debts of the world's poorest developing countries.

What's Next?

Not so long ago, the global economy was hailed as the greatest thing
on earth. Now U.S. Treasury Secretary Robert Rubin calls for a "new architecture" for the international financial system and Goldman Sachs International chair Peter Sutherland calls "existing organizations"
governing the global economy—including the G-7, the World Bank, and
the IMF—"inadequate" and proposes a "summit conference on globalization" to promote "a serious rethinking of how international institutions and world leaders cope with the stresses and strains of
globalization."[27]

The great majority of people in the United States and worldwide have
been excluded from participation and representation in decision-making
about the global economy. Instead of "one person one vote," we've seen
"one dollar one vote"—with one billionaire having the same influence as
a billion destitute people.

If "governments derive their just powers from the consent of the governed," the global political system today is fundamentally illegitimate.
We face a new global order that is not based on the consent of the governed. Governing structures at local, national, and global levels are
tainted by coercion, corruption, usurpation, and bias by and on behalf of
global corporations and privileged elites.

Creating a new architecture must not be a process in which the few
are the architects and the many merely day laborers who build the buildings but have no say in their design. Nor should it produce mansions for
the rich and hovels for everyone else. All the world's people have a right
to participate in shaping the "new architecture" of the global economy
and to share in its benefits.

We hope this new edition of *Global Village or Global Pillage* will help
people figure out how to exercise that right.

Introduction

All over the world, people are being pitted against each other to see who will offer global corporations the lowest labor, social, and environmental costs. Their jobs are being moved to places with inferior wages, lower business taxes, and more freedom to pollute. Their employers are using the threat of "foreign competition" to hold down wages, salaries, taxes, and environmental protections and to replace high-quality jobs with temporary, part-time, insecure, and low-quality jobs. Their government officials are justifying cuts in education, health, and other services as necessary to reduce business taxes in order to keep or attract jobs.

If you fear that the growing freedom of corporations to move jobs around the world threatens you and what you value, you are probably right. And you are in good company: Hundreds of millions of people all over the world face a similar threat. The purpose of this book is to stimulate dialogue on what these changes mean and how those they threaten can defend themselves and reassert control over their future. It is not a conventional book about economics written for specialists, but rather a book about people—how they are affected by globalization and what they can do about it.

Globalization

Battles over such once-esoteric international economic issues as the North American Free Trade Agreement (NAFTA) and the General Agreement on Tariffs and Trade (GATT) have moved from the business page to the front page. "Globalization" has become the buzzword-of-the-day—on the lips of politicians, professors, and pundits alike. Corporations, markets, finance, banking, transportation, communication, and production more and more cut across national boundaries. Globalization—the shorthand term we will use for this globalization of capital—is being deliberately accelerated by most national governments, by international institutions like the International Monetary Fund (IMF) and World Bank, and by the global corporations themselves. While international trade is nothing new, this rapid globalization of capital is an epochal change, creating what is often called the "New World Economy."

Globalization has made available some exotic products from all over the world, reduced some prices, and opened dazzling new opportunities for some people. It has immensely expanded the wealth and power of a few hundred global corporations. But for the majority of people in most parts of the world, the era of globalization has had its downsides. They have endured rising unemployment, falling real incomes, mass layoffs, cutbacks in public services, deteriorating working conditions, elimination of small farms and businesses, accelerating destruction of the environment, and loss of democratic control over their governments and societies.

While these problems have many causes, all are aggravated by globalization. An unregulated global economy forces workers, communities, and countries to compete to attract corporate investment. So each tries to reduce labor, social, and environmental costs below the others. The result is "downward leveling"—a disastrous "race to the bottom" in which conditions for all tend to fall toward those of the poorest and most desperate.

Downward leveling is in part an unintended consequence of millions of unconnected decisions made by individuals and businesses pursuing their private interests. But it is also a deliberate policy objective of global corporations, which have sought to impose a "Corporate Agenda" on local and national governments and international institutions. This Corporate Agenda aims to reduce all barriers to downward leveling of environmental, labor, and social costs. It has been incorporated in trade agreements like NAFTA and GATT, in World Bank and IMF policies of "shock therapy" and "structural adjustment," and in government policies that lower conditions for the majority in pursuit of "competitiveness."

Poverty, unemployment, inequality, corporate domination of government, economic stagnation, and environmental degradation are nothing new. For the past two centuries, the main vehicles that people have used to address such problems have been national governments and national social movements. But as corporations have become increasingly global, and as supranational institutions like the IMF, World Bank, and GATT have become increasingly powerful, these vehicles have grown less and less effective. The powers that people have established in the national arena have been largely outflanked by globalization. The result can be a pervasive feeling of powerlessness in the face of unaccountable global forces.

Globalization is an immensely complex process, involving virtually every aspect of global life. Much of that process is deliberately concealed—conducted in secret negotiations over trade agreements and corporate alliances and recorded in hidden corporate bookkeeping but not in the phony returns supplied to government tax authorities.[1] Future historians, though armed with documents kept from us, are still likely to debate at length what was actually going on in the era of globalization.

Meanwhile, those threatened by globalization need the best possible understanding of what is happening in order to respond. But the available knowledge is highly fragmented among different scholarly fields and diverse political discourses. This book draws on a wide range of recent writing in economics, history, political science, sociology and other fields, interviews and discussions with dozens of scholars and activists, and our own experience and observation, to illuminate how globalization affects ordinary people around the world and to explore the shifts it necessitates in social strategies. We hope the book will help reframe the discussion of globalization, making it easier for trade unionists and those concerned about Third World poverty, environmentalists and human rights advocates, policy analysts and community leaders to engage in a common dialogue.[2]

Resisting the New World Economy

For most of the world's people, the "New World Economy" is a disaster that is already happening. Those it hurts can't escape it. But neither can they afford to accept it. The result has been a widespread but little-recognized series of revolts against international trade agreements, austerity "shock therapy" and "structural adjustment" programs, loss of rights, reductions in living conditions, and other consequences of globalization. Just in the year before this book went to press:

- An unusual coalition of environmentalists, trade unionists, farmers, consumer advocates, and other citizen activists formed in the United States, Mexico, and Canada to oppose NAFTA. Against a unified front of business, all three governments, and the Democratic and Republican parties, they came within a few votes of defeating the pact in the U.S. Congress.

- Indigenous people organized as the Zapatista National Liberation Army seized the principal cities of the southern Mexican province of Chiapas. In addition to demands for democratization, land reform, and rights for indigenous peoples, they stated: "The North American Free Trade Agreement is the death certificate for the indigenous people of Mexico. We rose up in arms to respond to [Mexican President] Salinas' death sentence against our people."[3]

- Hundreds of thousands of French students and workers demonstrated and battled police to oppose a decree allowing young workers to be paid only 30 to 80 percent of the minimum wage. After weeks of disruption in major cities, the government withdrew the decree.[4]

- In the city of Bangalore, India, a half-million farmers joined a "seed satyagraha" to protest proposed provisions of GATT that they believed would allow global corporations to destroy their livelihood. They were addressed by representatives of farm and other organizations from Ethiopia, the Philippines, Sri Lanka, Malaysia, Thailand, Nicaragua, Brazil, Indonesia, Korea, and Zimbabwe who shared the same concern.[5]

- Workers in Belgium called a general strike, their first since 1936, to protest a government austerity package that froze real wages and cut welfare, health, and pension funds to restore "international competitiveness." The general strike crippled transportation, shipping, postal service, and public schools and closed down the offices of such global corporations as GM, Bayer, and BASF.[6]

- In Poland, the parties advocating economic "shock therapy" were voted out of office. When the new government failed to keep its campaign promises to increase wages and spend more on social welfare, 30,000 workers from all over Poland marched through Warsaw to protest.[7]

- Over a million Europeans joined coordinated demonstrations in 150 cities to protest rising unemployment. From London to Rome, workers struck to call attention to the loss of jobs.[8]

These events may appear unrelated, but they are not. While each has its unique local causes and character, these actions—and hundreds of similar actions in scores of other countries—are part of a little-recognized worldwide resistance to the effects of globalization. Whether the movements emanating from these actions protect narrow special interests, lash out in chauvinistic rage at political scapegoats, or take a more constructive direction will be crucial to the future of politics worldwide.

Globalization-from-Below

Globalization is generating more than just popular revolts. It is producing a common interest in resisting downward leveling among diverse constituencies. That is why struggles against the

New World Economy have brought about seemingly improbable alliances of environmentalists and labor unions; farmers and public health activists; advocates for human rights, women's rights, and Third World development; and others whose interests were once widely assumed to conflict.

Downward leveling similarly produces a common interest among people in different countries and regions of the world. In the logic of global competition, they should compete with each other to attract global capital by providing the cheapest environmental, social, and labor conditions. But downward leveling is opening the way for a different logic—a common interest in forestalling a race to the bottom.

New transnational networks are arising, based on such common interests. In North America, a "North American Worker-to-Worker Network" now links grassroots labor activists in Mexico, the United States, and Canada via conferences, tours, solidarity support, and a newsletter; "Mujer a Mujer" links women's groups to share successful strategies and search for alternative models of regional integration; community groups and trade unions have organized numerous meetings and tours to bring together Mexican and U.S. workers. In other parts of the world, parallel networks, such as the People's Plan 21 in the Asian-Pacific and Central American regions, and the Third World Network based in Penang, have been developing similar vehicles for transnational cooperation. Such efforts are creating an alternative to the globalization of capital—an alternative which might be called "globalization-from-below." [9]

A Human Agenda

These new transnational networks are now developing *transnational* programs to counter the effects of global economic restructuring.[10] While they may differ in emphases and details, these alternative programs all seek to provide environmentally and socially sustainable win/win solutions for ordinary people in different parts of the world. They are important not only because of the solutions they propose, but also because those solutions have emerged from a dialogue rooted in such a diversity of groups and experiences. They can serve as building blocks for a "Human Agenda," embodying interests that are widely shared by people all over the world but that are threatened by the Corporate Agenda.

Upward Leveling

In this book we make a preliminary effort to synthesize different alternatives to the Corporate Agenda into a common alternative. The core of that alternative is "upward leveling"—raising the standards of those at the bottom and thereby reducing their downward pull on everybody else. Upward leveling does not mean that everyone can or should live like the wealthiest citizens of the wealthiest countries—its goal is ecologically sustainable well-being for all, not conspicuous consumption and unsustainable waste. Nor does it mean uniformity of products and lifestyles: upward leveling is compatible with diversity among different cultural groups. But it does mean a cumulative increase in both power and well-being for the poorest and least powerful—poor and working people, women, marginalized groups, and their communities. The advancement of those at the bottom is crucial to blocking the race to the bottom.

Upward leveling requires grassroots rebellions against downward leveling, local coalition-building, transnational networking, and creating or reforming international institutions. We call the weaving together of these efforts the "Lilliput Strategy"— based on the way the tiny Lilliputians in *Gulliver's Travels* captured Gulliver, many times their size, by tying him with hundreds of threads while he slept. Only by combining their efforts can those resisting the effects of globalization in Chicago and Warsaw, Chiapas and Bangalore begin to bring the New World Economy under control.

The Chapters

The first four chapters of this book describe the process of globalization and its impact. Chapter One, "The Race to the Bottom," describes the dynamics of downward leveling and the "seven danger signals" of destructive globalization. Chapter

Two, "The Era of Nation-Based Economies," provides a brief primer on the relation between nation states and economies prior to globalization. Chapter Three, "The Dynamics of Globalization," explores the causes and forms of globalization and the paradigm shift necessary to understand them. Chapter Four, "The Flawed Debate," examines how pre-globalization concepts like "free trade," "protectionism," "economic nationalism," and "internationalism" have distorted discussion of the New World Economy, and how new paradigms, such as "globalization-from-below," have begun to emerge.

Chapters Five through Nine address how to correct the negative consequences of globalization. Chapter Five, "Resistance is Global," describes the varied forms of resistance to the effects of globalization that have emerged in underdeveloped, newly-industrialized, ex-Communist, and industrial countries, and the formation of transnational movements to challenge international institutions like the World Bank, IMF, NAFTA, and GATT. Chapter Six, "The Lilliput Strategy," discusses ways to bridge the divisions among economic philosophies, diverse social movements, rich and poor countries, and nation states in the worldwide movement against downward leveling. Chapter Seven, "Global Rules," describes a variety of means, including corporate codes of conduct, international labor and environmental rights campaigns, and social charters, to establish international rules to block downward leveling. Chapter Eight, "Labor in the New World Economy," examines the emergence of a new labor internationalism as one example of how an institution that has functioned primarily in the national arena can adapt to globalization. Chapter Nine, "Reversing the Race to the Bottom," integrates ideas from a variety of transnational coalitions into a draft of a "Human Agenda" based on combining grassroots economic initiatives with new forms of global regulation.

For those who wish to explore this subject further, we have included a resource listing of books, articles, periodicals, videos, and organizations.

Grassroots and Global

The authors of this book start with a strong orientation toward local, grassroots action. Twenty years ago when we collaborated on a book that examined the position of young workers in the United States and the various ways they attempted to affect their conditions,[11] at no point did we consider it necessary even to mention the international economy. Since then we have participated in and written about labor, environmental, economic development, community organizing, and other movements that have been highly local in their focus.[12] Gradually we have been forced to realize that the grassroots efforts we cherish so highly are likely to come to naught unless they "think locally and act globally."

This book is inevitably marked by our own limitations. While we have tried to present a global perspective, we have a disproportionate number of examples from the United States, simply because it is the country we know best. And while we believe that many movements are developing alternatives to the New World Economy, we have dealt most extensively with the labor movement—simply because we know more about it. We ask not that others forgive our limitations but that they take up the task of remedying them.

This book stresses the practical, interest-oriented aspects of globalization. But globalization also presents profound ethical and even spiritual challenges. Shall we dedicate our lives to individual acquisition? Shall we define ourselves in terms of narrow interest or identity groups? Or shall we seek broader solidarities with other beings around the planet? In the era of globalization, aiding others may be the prerequisite to saving ourselves.

Like it or not, our lives and our children's lives will be lived in the global economy. We'd better fix it.

Chapter One

The Race to the Bottom

Two decades ago, David Rockefeller of Chase Manhattan Bank proclaimed, "Broad human interests are being served best in economic terms where free market forces are able to transcend national boundaries."[1]

This theme has since been echoed and re-echoed. For example, a report on "The Case for Free Trade" published by the Twentieth Century Fund in 1989 stated "all nations will benefit from multilateral liberalization."[2] And in his 1994 State of the Union address, President Bill Clinton described the global market as the key to the U.S. economic future. "It means jobs and rising living standards for the American people—low deficits, low inflation, low interest rates, low trade barriers and high investments."[3]

We hear the following simple argument for the benefits of globalization again and again. When "free market forces are able to transcend national boundaries," tariffs, subsidies, and other "artificial" barriers are removed and efficient firms rewarded. Countries will specialize in those products they make most cheaply. Greater efficiency leads to lower prices. *Everybody bene-*

fits. Politicians, economists, and media often repeat this credo as if it were not faith but fact.[4]

Unfortunately, in the real world this cheerful theory has a problem: as corporations "transcend national boundaries" they can force workers, communities, and countries to compete to lower labor, social, and environmental costs—force them into a "race to the bottom":

- BMW announces that it plans to build an auto factory in the United States. Several states bid for the plant. Ultimately South Carolina, notorious for its low wages, lax enforcement of environmental laws, and suppression of unions, offers BMW a $300 million subsidy for land, road, water, sewer, office, housing, airport, training, and other costs. BMW builds its plant in South Carolina. The company's employment costs are $12-16 per hour, compared to $25 per hour in Germany. Comments *Financial World* magazine, "The message will likely not be lost on German unions, should they threaten to strike BMW."[5]

- The British Department of Trade and Industry sets up a special office called "Invest in Britain." It advertises in German business newspapers that Britain offers a top corporate tax rate of 33 percent compared to 50 percent in Germany and labor costs 78 percent below those in Germany. One advertisement reports that a thousand firms have moved to Britain to take advantage of low wages and social contributions.[6]

- London International Group P.L.C., manufacturer of surgical gloves and condoms, closes three British plants and eliminates 1,000 jobs. "London International is seeking to shift production from Britain to lower-cost production plants in Asia."[7]

- In South Korea and Taiwan, economic growth, democratic reforms, and unionization lead to rising wages. So Nike closes down 20 footwear factories there and contracts to have Nikes made in China, Thailand, and Indonesia. In Indonesia, the girls and young women workers start at $1.35 per day. In 1992, the entire annual payroll for the Indonesian factories that make Nikes was less than Michael Jordan's reported $20 million fee for promoting them. The Nikes cost $5.60 a pair to produce in Indonesia; they sell in the United States for $45 to $80 a pair.[8]

- The Johnson Tombigbee Furniture Manufacturing Company finds labor, environmental, and workplace health-and-safety costs too high in its home town of Columbus, Mississippi. So it starts making the parts for its furniture in Honduras, the Philippines, and Brazil. It has a chair made in Brazil for $12.50, which it sells in the United States for about $50. It recently received a bid from China to make the same chair for $4.50. Company head T. Scott Berry muses, "Where is cheap labor and massive amounts of raw material? I thought it was Brazil, but now it looks like it's China." *The New York Times* headlines its article about the offer "For a Furniture Maker, a Taste of a Global Future."[9]

The New World Economy

Modern capitalism developed within a system of territorial states. Trade and investment between countries were important, but they were usually conducted by companies rooted in one home country. Some companies had large holdings in foreign countries, but usually as part of an imperialism in which ultimate control remained "at home." National governments controlled treasury departments, central banks, trade and labor policies, taxation, commercial law, and other key economic institutions and thereby shaped their national economies.

This system of nation-based economies is rapidly evolving toward a global economy. Computer, communication, and transportation technologies have lessened distance as a barrier, making possible the coordination of production and commerce on a global scale. Lowered tariffs have reduced national frontiers as barriers to commerce, facilitating transnational production and distribution. Corporations are globalizing not only to reduce production costs, but also to expand markets, evade taxes, acquire knowledge and resources, and protect themselves against currency fluctuations and other risks. As Robert B. Reich, now U.S. Secretary of Labor, wrote in 1991, "As almost every factor of production—money, technology, factories, and equipment—moves effortlessly across borders, the very idea of an American economy is becoming meaningless, as are the notions of an American corporation, American capital, American products, and American technology. A similar transformation is affecting every other nation."[10]

Three hundred companies now own an estimated one-quarter of the productive assets of the world.[11] Of the top 100 economies in the world, 47 are corporations—each with more wealth than 130 countries.[12] Their interests are global: as *The New York Times* noted in 1989, "Many American companies are shedding the banner of national identity and proclaiming themselves to be global enterprises whose fortunes are no longer so dependent on the economy of the United States."[13]

Such global corporations have formed complex alliances that blur the very boundaries of the firm. In the automobile industry, Ford owns 25 percent of Mazda; GM and Toyota are involved in a joint venture; GM owns part of a Fiat subsidiary in the United States; Fiat owns 48 percent of Ford's Iveco Truck subsidiary. Nissan produces a VW in Japan, while in Brazil and Argentina, VW and Ford have combined operations in a joint venture called Autolatina. Such alliances do not mean that these companies do not compete—only that they also cooperate.[14]

Production increasingly takes place in a "global factory" where different phases of production are performed in different countries. When an American buys a Pontiac Le Mans from General Motors for $10,000, for example, "$3,000 goes to South Korea for routine labor and assembly operations, $1,750 to Japan for advanced components (engines, transaxles, and electronics), $750 to West Germany for styling and design engineering, $400 to Taiwan, Singapore, and Japan for small components, $250 to Britain for advertising and marketing services, and about $50 to Ireland and Barbados for data processing."[15]

Capital and financial markets have become global and the foreign exchange market processes approximately $1 trillion per day.[16] Since 1983, global foreign direct investment has grown at an average of 29 percent a year, three times faster than the growth of export trade and four times the growth of world output.[17] According to one expert on world monetary systems, "Some individual currency speculators have as much money as some small countries."[18]

International economic institutions like the IMF, the World Bank, the European Union (EU), and GATT have developed powers formerly reserved for nation states. Conversely, national governments have become less and less able to control their own economies; they are more and more like flotsam tossed on the waves of global economic forces—witness the inability of central banks, even acting in concert, to control the repeated currency crises of the 1990s.

This economic globalization is part of a wider historical transformation.[19] Not only do products and money stream across national boundaries, but also satellite broadcasts, greenhouse gasses, and fleeing refugees. The growth of a realm beyond the control of individual nations poses fundamental challenges to democracy and the nation-state system—and to ordinary citizens.

This epochal change requires a corresponding shift in perspective. In the New World Economy it is no longer sufficient to address the problems of a single country. We need to understand—and to control—economic processes that are now global.

Downward Leveling

In a competitive market, sales generally go to the competitor who offers the lowest price. As a result, prices tend toward the level of the lowest cost producer. When this tendency lowers the price of goods and services through the improved efficiency touted by the advocates of free-market forces, the effect may be benign. But when corporations and governments lower costs by reducing environmental protection, wages, salaries, health care, and education, the result can be malignant—a "downward leveling" of environmental, labor, and social conditions.

Farmers, workers, consumers, and citizens threatened by downward leveling have long organized themselves locally and nationally to resist malignant effects of competition. They have encouraged governments to adopt environmental, labor, and social policies that block downward leveling. But corporations can now outflank the controls governments and organized citizens once placed on them by relocating their facilities around the world.

Today, if governments and workforces fail to provide labor, social, economic, and regulatory conditions to corporations' liking, corporations can just go elsewhere—leaving economic devastation in their wake. Says T. Scott Berry of Johnston Tombigbee Furniture Company, for example, "I see my furniture being made mostly of foreign-made parts... With all the growing government intervention in manufacturing, whether it's the EPA, OSHA, workers' comp, we'll get to the point where we'll be an assembler and packager."[20] Or corporations can simply *threaten* to go elsewhere. Workers, communities, and countries then seem to have little choice but to compete for corporate favor: If Korea restricts environmental pollution, allows union organization, raises wages, and taxes corporations to pay for health and education, Nike can simply shift its footwear production to Indonesia. By promoting suppliers in less developed countries, Nike deliberately "keeps pressure on" producers "to keep production costs low as developing sources mature."[21]

Tan Chuan Ceng, who owns a factory in Indonesia making shoes for Reebok at $10.20 per pair, says, "Even if all the Reebok producers got together and went to Reebok and said, 'Give me $13 for these so we can pay workers more,' it wouldn't work. I think they would say, 'We'll go to China and pay $8.'" The head of Reebok's Indonesian operations acknowledges, "Cutting costs is part of our business. It's difficult for anybody to compete with China because wages there present a tremendous competitive factor."[22]

Downward leveling is not limited to low-skill, low-tech jobs; it increasingly affects high-skilled professionals. A software programming center in Bangalore, India, services thirty global corporations, including Microsoft, Digital, Fujitsu, Bull, Olivetti, Oracle, IBM, and Motorola, at half the price the same work would cost in the United States or Western Europe. Metropolitan Life employs 150 workers in County Cork, Ireland, to examine medical claims from all over the world; costs are one-third below the United States, and the Irish Development Authority provides tax and other incentives. Computer programmers work in Gdansk, Poland for a U.S. communications equipment maker who pays them a fraction of comparable U.S. salaries.[23] Company officials can communicate with such employees across the world by satellite as easily as they can communicate with workers in the building next door.

Downward leveling affects people in all parts of the world and in rich and poor countries alike. Loss of job security in the United States, growing unemployment in Europe, mushrooming poverty in the Third World, falling living standards in Eastern Europe and the former Soviet Union, and denial of human and labor rights in much of Asia are all aggravated by downward leveling. The force that drives BMW to move jobs from Germany to South Carolina drives the Johnson Tombigbee Furniture Company to move jobs from Mississippi to Brazil and then to China. As Princeton economist William Baumol puts it, "It is not that foreigners are stealing our jobs, it is that we are all facing one another's competition."[24]

Of course, globalization is not the source of all the world's ills. Poverty, unemployment, disease, environmental degradation, injustice, and oppression have deep roots in local social structures and even in plain human cussedness. Nonetheless, downward leveling is like a cancer that is destroying its host organism—the earth and its people. Notwithstanding the many other factors at work, this underlying disease will progress until it receives treatment. Its symptoms may have been masked for a time, but today its malignant effects on people and the environment are increasingly apparent in the United States and throughout the world. They range from falling wages and loss of job security to global warming and paralysis of democratic government. We might summarize those symptoms as the "seven danger signals" of a cancerous, out-of-control global economy:

- ## Race to the Bottom

    The most direct symptom of globalization is the "race to the bottom" itself—the reduction in labor, social, and environmental conditions that results directly from global competition for jobs and investment. Sometimes the immediate vehicle is a corporation that itself threatens to close or move unless workers and/or governments accept the conditions it demands. Sometimes the race to the bottom is promoted by a government—as when the government of Spain tried to reduce job security regulations in 1994 in order to make its workforce "more competitive." Sometimes it is imposed by international financial institutions—as when countries are denied loans by the IMF and World Bank unless they agree to reduce minimum wages and raise food costs as part of a "structural adjustment program."

    In the late 1980s, an article in *The New York Times* noted that "competition from foreign producers" had become a "chief bargaining card" for employers going into labor negotiations. It quoted Stanley Mihelick, executive vice president of the Goodyear Company, as saying, "Until we get real wage levels down much closer to those of the Brazils or Koreas, we cannot pass along productivity gains to wages and still be competitive."[25] And in fact, real wage levels in the United States have been moving closer to "those of the Brazils and the Koreas." Real wages have declined about 15 percent since 1973. Real incomes for young families decreased by one-third from 1973 to 1991.[26] Even for such a favored group as college-educated men in the prime earning years of 45 to 54, median real income fell by 17 percent between 1986 and 1992.[27] The new jobs opening up in the mid-1990s "come with wages typically below $8 an hour, or about $16,000 a year, and without health benefits, much opportunity for promotion, or promises that the jobs will last."[28]

Such social benefits as publicly subsidized housing, transportation, education, and health care have also been slashed: 60 percent of the unemployed do not receive unemployment compensation and 38 million people are without any form of health insurance. Despite the near doubling of productivity since 1973, the time necessary for an American worker paid the average hourly wage to earn the average household's yearly expenses has grown by 43 percent; to buy the average new house by 45 percent; and to pay for a year at the University of California by 75 percent.[29]

Job security has become more the exception than the rule as corporations, in the name of "competitiveness," have replaced union seniority systems and stable job structures with "flexibility" and subcontracting. Since 1982, temporary employment has increased 250 percent; in 1993, temporary employment accounted for two-thirds of new private sector jobs.[30] Over 20 percent of American jobs are part-time or temporary—so-called "contingent jobs"—the highest proportion ever.[31] Familes of part-time workers are six times as likely to live in poverty.[32]

Into the contingent workforce have been crowded those who face discrimination in U.S. society: people of color, women, immigrants, the young, and the elderly. Two-thirds of all part-timers and 60 percent of all temporary workers are women.[33]

Paradoxically, those who are employed full-time are working significantly longer hours and/or taking extra jobs. According to economist Juliet Schor, the average employed person worked 163 more hours in 1987 than in 1969—equal to an extra month of work.[34] Illegal employment of children under fourteen almost tripled between 1983 and 1992.[35] Workplace health and safety inspection has been cut to the minimum, leading to industrial accidents reminiscent of the 19th century, such as the deaths of dozens of poultry factory workers in a fire in Hamlet, North Carolina, where factory doors were locked to keep workers inside. Work at all levels has been subject to speed-up as union work rules have been dismantled, "flexible" work processes introduced, and workers deprived of any protection against threats of unjustified discharge.

In the Third World the trends are similar but more severe. Almost one-third of the population of the developing countries, 1.3 billion people, live in absolute poverty—too poor to provide the minimum diet required for full human functioning.[36] It is often argued that foreign investment will raise wages in poor countries. But a review of U.S. corporate behavior abroad by the *Boston Globe* found that "rather than raising standards of living, American firms are more likely to be paying no better than local minimum wages." A study sponsored by the International Labor Organization found that in Indonesia—now a favorite spot for companies like Nike and Reebok—88 percent of women earning the Indonesian minimum wage were malnourished.[37]

What about the "success stories" of the New World Economy—the "Newly Industrialized Countries" [NICs], such as the East Asian "Tigers"? They have seen great economic growth, largely based on the exploitation of labor and the unsustainable destruction of the environment.[38] The benefits have often, though not always, been restricted to a small elite. But even these countries are far from immune to the race to the bottom. T.C. Lee, a banker at Citibank in Taipei, noted that in Taiwan, "there are lots of labor-intensive industries—garments, shoes, toys. All of them started to look outside to invest. They started to relocate initially to Thailand, Indonesia, Malaysia, and in the last two years, China, to enjoy cheap labor, cheap land, cheap living costs." Michael M.C. Lin, president of a conglomerate corporation in Taiwan, built a furniture factory in China. "Labor costs were the most important thing for us," he said.[39]

The race to the bottom is contributing to environmental destruction worldwide. Global corporations' oil refineries, steel mills, chemical plants, and other factories, now located all over the world, are the main source of greenhouse gases, ozone-depleting chemicals, and toxic pollutants. Their packaging is a major source of solid waste. Overfishing of the world's waters, overcutting of forests, and the destructive use of land result both from the search for higher corporate profits and the increase in poverty, which leads to desperate overharvesting of natural resources.

The 7,000 Philippine islands, for example, were "lavishly endowed with rainforests, fish, fertile low-lands, and extensive mineral deposits" as recently as World War II. Today, "there are few places you can go in the Philippines without meeting some sort of ecological disaster." In one part of Mindanao, "the forests were thick, and the people few. Now, thanks to the greed of the big commercial logging companies and the need of the small agriculturalists (who move into the forests only after the loggers have built roads and chopped down the biggest trees), the mountains are almost bare." The proportion of the Philippines that is forested has decreased from 35 percent to 20 percent—less than half the amount needed to maintain a stable ecosystem—just since 1969.[40]

- Downward Spiral

The race to the bottom has unintended side effects that multiply its impact. As each workforce, community, or country seeks to become "more competitive" by reducing its wages and social and environmental overheads, incomes and social and material infrastructures deteriorate. Lower wages and reduced public spending mean less buying power, leading to stagnation, recession, and unemployment. As corporations move jobs that paid $10 per hour to countries where they pay $1 per hour, workers can buy less of what they produce. As each country tries to solve its own problems by producing and exporting still more products still more cheaply, the result is a "downward spiral." This dynamic is aggravated by the accumulation of debt, as poor countries and even the United States gear their economies to debt repayment at the expense of consumption, investment, and development.

This downward spiral is reflected in the slowing of global GNP growth from almost 5 percent per year from 1948 to 1973 to only half that in the 1974 to 1989 period and to a mere crawl since then. (The deterioration would be even greater if such non-GNP factors as degradation of the world's land, air, and water were factored in.)

In the United States during the 1980s, factory closings led to mass unemployment and the creation of the "Rust Belt" in the industrial midwest. Despite alleged "economic recovery," manufacturing jobs fell more than 8 percent from 1989 to the start of 1994.[41] Since weekly wages average $500 in manufacturing but only $350 in the service sector, elimination of factory jobs means lower incomes.[42]

In the face of global competition, companies have increasingly turned to "corporate downsizing" in an effort to become "lean and mean." Downsizing is affecting almost every sector of the economy and white- as well as blue-collar workers. In 1993 and 1994, "service" companies like Sears, Roebuck, BankAmerica, AT&T, and Aetna joined manufacturers like General Electric, Xerox, and Procter & Gamble in massive permanent layoffs.[43] Even highly profitable companies in high technology growth industries are downsizing: The telecommunications industry laid off 60,000 workers in 1993.[44] As a result, according to *Business Week*, "Today's corporation is no longer a secure or stable place... Fear is almost palpable in the corridors of the reengineered workplace, where loyalty takes a backseat to survival and personal achievement."[45]

According to MIT economist Lester Thurow, "In the United States, if one adds together the officially unemployed, discouraged workers who have stopped actively searching for work and those with part-time jobs who want full-time work, 15 percent of the labor force (19 million) is looking for work."[46] In a February 1994 poll, one-quarter of those questioned said they had personally experienced lay-offs, pay cuts, or reductions in hours in the previous two years, and two-fifths worried that they might be laid off or forced to take pay cuts in the next two years.[47] An official unemployment rate of 6 percent is now widely accepted as "full employment."[48] While more education is sometimes touted as the solution, Dan Hecker of the U.S. Bureau of Labor Statistics says, "We're getting more college graduates than we are college-level jobs. About 20 percent of the college graduates end up in non-college-level jobs."[49]

The effects of the downward spiral are global. In 1993, President Clinton quite unexpectedly acknowledged that there was a "global crisis of unemployment." He noted, "All the advanced nations are having difficulty creating new jobs, even when their economies are growing...We have to figure out how to unlock the doors for people who are left behind in this new global economy." In Europe and Canada unemployment has risen to 11 percent; it is at historic highs in Japan; it probably runs from 20 to 40 percent in most ex-Communist countries.[50] In the United States, unemployment remained near its recession peak after several years of "jobless recovery"; more than 60 percent of the new jobs created in 1993 were part-time. For the 24 industrialized countries of the Organization for Economic Cooperation and Development (OECD), the official unemployment rate is 8.5 percent—a "reserve army" of 35 million. According to United Nations estimates, there are some 700 million people currently unemployed or underemployed in the developing world. The International Labor Organization (ILO) projects that global unemployment will reach one billion in 1994.[51]

The downward spiral is also manifested in other ways. In the former Communist states of Eastern Europe and the Soviet Union, death rates have risen and birth rates have fallen precipitously. Infant mortality is rising in Russia, Bulgaria, Latvia, Moldova, Romania, and Ukraine.[52] A study of "Structural Adjustment and the Determinants of Poverty in Latin America" prepared for the InterAmerican Development Bank found that "the harsh structural adjustments of the 1980s have significantly worsened the poverty problem. Casual evidence from virtually every country confirms the deterioration of living standards and the widening inequality of the last decade."[53] Africa's GNP fell by an average of 2.2 percent per year in the 1980s.[54] In African countries with IMF-World Bank programs, spending on health decreased by 50 percent and on education by 25 percent during the 1980s.[55] A United Nations advisory group reported that throughout Africa, "health systems are collapsing for lack of medicines, schools have no books, and universities suffer from a debilitating lack of library and laboratory facilities."[56]

In rich and poor countries alike, economic insecurity, disruption, and poverty have undermined human relationships, traditional lifeways, and social values. A California lawyer recently wrote,

> I am a criminal defense lawyer, not an economist, but I wish to reinject into the discussion what strikes me as self-evident: The lack of decent-paying work for our unskilled and semi-skilled workforce is a major cause of United States crime and social decay. The bulk of my clientele falls into the chronically unemployed and the newly laid off or chronically under-employed. The gainfully employed mostly do not commit crimes. The remaining, and growing, portion, who are not securely employed or decently paid need solid factory jobs to work their way out of poverty, and those jobs don't exist anymore. Why? Because they've been moved...Now we cannot employ all our people at a living wage, and as a result, our nation is suffering a catastrophic decline in living standards with an unravelling of our social fabric. [57]

- ## Polarization of Haves and Have-nots

While globalization is often portrayed as a game in which everyone wins, even official economists now have to admit otherwise. Laura D'Andrea Tyson, chair of President Clinton's Council of Economic Advisors, acknowledges that "Globalization has depressed the wage growth of low-wage workers. It's been a reason for the increasing wage gap between high-wage and low-wage workers."[58] Globalization hits especially hard at racial and ethnic minorities concentrated in manufacturing: A study of 80,000 Chicago manufacturing jobs lost during the 1980s due to plant closings or major layoffs by transnational corporations and their subsidiaries found that over half were lost by people of color.[59] As National Urban League President Hugh Price put it, "The manufacturing jobs that once enabled blue collar workers to purchase their own homes and occasional new cars have all but vanished from the inner city"; and while racism is still abroad in the land, "the global realignment of work and wealth is, if anything, the bigger culprit."[60]

In the U.S., the 1 percent with the highest incomes nearly doubled their share of national income from 8 percent in 1980 to 14.7 percent in 1989.[61] The top 1 percent increased their share of wealth from 27 percent in the 1970s to 36 percent at the end of the 1980s.[62] The net worth of the four hundred richest Americans trebled from $92 billion in 1982 to $270 billion in 1989.[63] Meanwhile, one-quarter of all infants and toddlers live in poverty,[64] including more than half of all black children under six. [65]

The gap between rich and poor is increasing worldwide. According to the United Nations Development Program's *Human Development Report 1992*, in 1970 the richest fifth of the world's people received 30 times more income than the bottom fifth; by 1989 they received nearly 60 times more. As a result, the richest fifth now receive more than 80 percent of the world's income, while the poorest fifth receive 1.4 percent.[66]

From 1982 through 1990, debtor countries in the South have paid their creditors in the North six-and-a-half billion dollars in interest and another six billion dollars in principal payments *per month*—as much as the entire Third World spends on education and health.[67] Yet the debtor country debts were 60 percent greater in 1990 than in 1982.[68]

• Loss of Democratic Control

Globalization has reduced the power of individuals and communities to shape their destinies through participation in democratic processes. The ability of governments to pursue development, full employment, or other national economic goals has been undermined by the power of capital to pick up and leave. Governmental economic power has been further weakened throughout the world by political movements expressing the Corporate Agenda of dismantling government institutions for regulating national economies. Trade agreements such as NAFTA and GATT further restrict national, state, and local governments. Walter Wriston, former chairman of Citicorp, describes how currency traders seated in front of "200,000 monitors in trading rooms all over the world" now conduct "a kind of global plebiscite on the monetary and fiscal policies of the governments issuing currency." This system is "far more draconian than any previous arrangement, such as the gold standard or the Bretton Woods system, since there is no way for a nation to opt out " Wriston gives as an example the election of President Francois Mitterand as an "ardent socialist" in 1981. "The market took one look at his policies and within six months the capital flight forced him to reverse course."[69] A senior Clinton advisor echoed his point in 1994: "The value of the dollar on any given day is like a global referendum on all the policies of the Clinton Administration combined. It is as though the world were having a huge discussion on the Internet, and the dollar's value is a snapshot of that discussion."[70] (Of course, those without the wealth to speculate don't count as part of "the world.")

The loss of democratic control is even greater in Third World debtor countries that have been subjected to structural adjustment programs. A recent series in *The New York Times* describes the World Bank and IMF as "the overlords of Africa." "For more than a decade the economies of Africa have been caught in a relentless downward spiral." As a result, African countries are finding themselves "more than ever under the thumb of outside powers." The IMF and the World Bank are "the purveyors of the new orthodoxy. They come in to bail out a country that is bankrupt. They do so by drawing up a 'structural adjustment program,' a tight package of economic prescriptions designed to bring about free market enterprise and minimum governmental interference." The Times concludes that through these programs, "the IMF and the bank now effectively oversee and supervise the economies of some 30 countries in sub-Saharan Africa."[71]

The inability of nations to control their own economies is undermining democratic political institutions. The various political crises and regime instabilities in much of Africa, Latin America, Asia, the ex-Communist countries, and Japan, France,

Germany, Italy, Canada, the United Kingdom and the United States—seemingly due to unrelated local factors—are actually in considerable part results of governments' inability to control national economies in the face of a crisis-ridden globalization.

- ## Uncontrolled Global Corporations

    Global corporations have become the world's most powerful economic actors, yet there are no international equivalents to the anti-trust, consumer protection, and other laws that provide a degree of corporate accountability at the national level. International capital mobility eliminates the long-term stake corporations once had in the well-being of their home nations. As Cyrill Siewert, a chief financial officer of Colgate-Palmolive, put it, "The United States does not have an automatic call on our resources. There is no mind-set that puts this country first."[72] The Bank of Commerce and Credit International scandals reveal just how much "freedom" global corporations have to engage in anti-social, not to say downright criminal, activity.

- ## Unaccountable Global Institutions

    The loss of national economic control has been accompanied by a growing concentration of power without accountability in international institutions like the IMF, the World Bank, and GATT. For poor countries, foreign control has been formalized in structural adjustment programs, but IMF decisions and GATT rules affect all countries. The decisions of these institutions also have an enormous impact on the global ecology—many environmentally destructive mega-projects in the Third World are financed by the World Bank, and GATT rules have been used to challenge such environmental measures as U.S. laws protecting dolphins. Yet these institutions represent a sphere of decisionmaking largely beyond the influence of citizens and citizen movements in poor and rich countries alike.

- ## Global Conflict

    Economic globalization is producing not global harmony, but rather a chaotic and destructive global rivalry. Despite their loss of economic autonomy, many nations remain armed and dangerous. In a swirl of self-contradictory strategies, major powers and global corporations use global institutions like GATT to impose open markets on their rivals, they pursue trade wars against each other, and they construct competing regional blocs like the European Union and NAFTA.

Such conflicts can easily become militarized. The 1992 draft *Defense Planning Guidance*, prepared by the U.S. Department of Defense but quickly disavowed by political leaders, stated that the United States must continue to dominate the international system by "discouraging the advanced industrialized nations from challenging our leadership or even aspiring to a larger global or regional role." Taking on this responsibility would ensure "a market-oriented zone of peace and prosperity that encompasses more than two-thirds of the world's economy."[73] In past eras, the rivalries growing from such perspectives have ultimately led to world war.

Globalization and its economic effects are also aggravating racism and extremist nationalism around the world. From the neo-Nazi skinheads of Germany to the "culture war" of Pat Buchanan, economic problems are being blamed not on the economic system or those who control it but on racial, ethnic, religious, and national scapegoats. Yugoslavia was reeling under an IMF shock therapy program just before its "ethnic cleansing" broke out; ethnic conflict in Rwanda had been aggravated by a World Bank project that shifted the economic balance between Hutu and Tutsi tribes. As with fascism in the 1930s, such chauvinism threatens not only those directly attacked, but the whole of society.

Global Village or Global Pillage?

Today, as David Rockefeller so fervently hoped twenty years ago, "free-market forces" are indeed "able to transcend national boundaries"—and to do so more easily than at any time in history. But it is questionable—at least based on the facts presented in this chapter—that "broad human interests" are thereby "being served best."

It is often said that globalization is leading to a global village. It would perhaps be more apt to say that globalization in its present form is leading to a pillage of the planet and its people.[74]

The 1990s have been full of happy talk about how "economic recovery" is under way. And indeed, this decade has been good for some. In 1993, for example, profits for the 500 largest U.S. manufacturing and service companies grew 14 percent— four times more than sales. But the benefits do not necessarily trickle down: For example, from March 1991 to the end of 1993 these same companies announced cutbacks of 10 percent in their total workforces—despite the ongoing "economic recovery."[75] A survey of the chief executive officers (CEOs) in 23 corporations that have each laid off more than 10,000 workers in the past three years found that their average CEO's compensation (not including stock options) rose 30 percent to about $1.9 million in 1993.[76]

Indeed, the New World Economy is characterized by such incongruities as jobless recoveries, the downsizing of highly profitable companies, and economic growth accompanied by falling wages and a growing "contingent" workforce. More of this kind of economic growth is highly unlikely to reverse the downward leveling described in this chapter.

Paradoxically, globalization is indeed serving "broad human interests"—but in a very different way than David Rockefeller ever imagined. One of the most important effects of globalization is one of the least recognized: Downward leveling is creating a lose-lose, negative-sum game for the majority of people in all parts of the world. Far from all winning, in a race to the bottom nearly all lose. As a result, the most diverse people share a common interest in halting the race to the bottom.

A desire to halt the race to the bottom implies neither a narrow, chauvinistic viewpoint nor a return to the nation-based economies of the past. There are other alternatives, including the "globalization-from-below" approach articulated in this book.

Chapter Two

The Era of Nation-Based Economies

Globalization represents an epochal change, but it is not the first epochal change that human beings have ever had to deal with. One way to begin to understand globalization is to consider it as the latest phase in the long history of changing relations between the political and economic dimensions of life. In this chapter we survey the relation between nation states and economies over the past few hundred years; in the next we identify some of the changes made by today's globalization. Such a review indicates the paradigm shift needed to understand globalization; it can also double as a primer on the arcane history, concepts, and jargon of international economics, from free trade and protectionism to capital mobility and comparative advantage, not to mention the IMF, structural adjustment programs, and GATT.

Politics and Economics

From the beginning of human existence, people have organized themselves into groups—initially families, tribes, and communities; later states and nations—with ways to determine the life of the group and its relation to others. They have also had to transform the world as they found it—to work—in order to live. The "political" and the "economic" aspects of human existence have interacted in diverse and changing ways through the course of human history.

Some of what human groups have produced with their labor they have used themselves; but from quite early in human development, part has gone to others as a free gift, as forced tribute, or as voluntary exchange. The excavations of ancient archeological sites reveal the remains of goods brought thousands of miles by ship, caravan, and human back. The goods thus conveyed ranged from spices and precious metals to human slaves.

Over the course of human history, different peoples have developed very diverse political and economic institutions. The nation-state system and the capitalist system emerged out of the feudal system of medieval Europe. Because they dominate the world today—and because they are the systems being transformed by today's globalization—their origin can provide a starting point for our story.[1]

States and Markets

Medieval Europe was governed by a multi-level political system in which monarchs shared law-making power and legitimate allegiance with feudal lords below them and the Holy Roman Emperor and Roman Catholic Church above. A "patchwork of overlapping and incomplete rights of government" were "inextricably superimposed and tangled."[2] Markets were extremely limited; most economic activity was controlled by feudal lords, whose peasants produced for them directly, or by guilds of craftsmen.

Within this system, markets, trade, and a class of capitalists gradually grew. At the same time, monarchs began to assert a monopoly of power within their realms. The budding capitalists found a territorially centralized organization increasingly useful for protecting property rights at home and abroad, while monarchs found growing capitalist wealth an important source of revenue for their emerging states. By the 17th century, the medieval multi-layered patchwork of political power had been replaced by a system of territorial states exercising a monopoly of power against church and feudal authorities within their territories and sovereignty against emperor and Pope. This system of territorial states whose rulers assert absolute sovereignty and independence has dominated international relations ever since.[3]

The emerging system of markets and capitalists had an ambiguous relation to the system of territorial states. Many capitalists traded internationally, but most also developed close ties with their "home" states, each providing support to the other. According to historical sociologist Michael Mann, by the time of the Industrial Revolution, "capitalism was already contained within a civilization of competing geopolitical states." Each of the leading European states "approximated a self-contained economic network," and economic interaction was largely confined within national boundaries—and each nations' imperial dominions.[4] European states shaped trade, often aiding it by national policies, war, and empire. By the 20th century, Europe and its offshoots like the United States—what came to be known as "the West"—controlled most of the world.

Democracy

Initially only very small classes and elites had any influence within the emerging territorial states. Gradually those excluded began to demand representation in the state. The idea of democratic self-government arose in conflict with monarchical domination and usually took the form of demanding that state rulers be selected by the people, who thereby would become citizens rather than subjects. In the "age of democratic revolutions," revolutions and insurrectionary movements in North America, France, Great Britain, and elsewhere replaced existing states with more democratic ones or forced existing states to provide vehicles for popular representation.

Even in democratic countries, most people remained excluded from control over economic institutions. In the 19th and 20th centuries, movements arose among the excluded groups and classes to extend democratic control over markets and enterprises either directly or via the state.

Nationalism

The people ruled by early modern states were often ethnically diverse, geographically scattered, and culturally unconnected with their rulers—a German could be King of England, for example. Starting around the late 18th century, however, nationalist movements began seeking to align states as territorial power centers with nations as communities of people who asserted common linguistic, racial, ethnic, religious, or historical bonds. In the nationalist view, humanity was assumed to be divided into distinct peoples. Each people was entitled to form a nation which in turn was entitled to a monopoly of political authority within a given territory. The sovereignty of states, originally conceived as "the divine right of kings," was redefined as a right of peoples.

From both a nationalist and a democratic perspective, the nation state was defined as the embodiment of the will of the people—meaning the citizens of the nation. The nation was generally presumed to possess a collective "national interest" which included the common interests of all ethnic subgroups and of different social classes.

Industrialism

A series of industrial revolutions, from the invention of machine production to today's computer-based technologies, immensely increased human productive capacity. The increased production was and remains controlled primarily by capitalist corporations, which organized an ever-increasing proportion of the world's economic activity. The size of these corporations grew exponentially. By the mid-20th century a small number of giant corporations, integrating all aspects of production from raw materials to the consumer, dominated major markets in each major country. A growing proportion of people became their employees.

Free Trade and Protectionism

Early modern European states pursued a policy known as "mercantilism" in which governments gave strong support to their merchants' efforts to sell abroad and accumulate wealth at home. In the wake of the first industrial revolution, British economists like Adam Smith and David Ricardo challenged mercantilism and advocated a system in which governments would not interfere with exchange among the enterprises of different countries. They argued that the wealth of all countries would be increased if each specialized in those products in which it had a "comparative advantage" that allowed it to produce more cheaply than others. People in Iceland should not try to produce bananas, but rather catch fish and exchange them with banana-growers in Honduras. This doctrine came to be known as "laissez-faire," "free trade," or "liberalism."[5] In the 19th century Britain adopted free trade and pressured other countries to do so, too.

Free trade was criticized, however, by economists in countries like Germany and the United States that industrialized later than Britain. They argued that a less industrialized country could never catch up unless it kept out products from already-industrialized countries: The products of new domestic industries would initially be costlier than those of established foreign industries, so people would buy imports instead of products made at home. They saw free trade as a way for strong, developed economies to permanently dominate weaker, less developed ones. Alexander Hamilton, George Washington's chief economic advisor, called for subsidies to protect the fledgling United States' "infant industries" from foreign competition.[6]

Many aspects of trade policy—especially high vs. low tariffs—divided the United States from its founding until World War II. Some agricultural interests and international merchants wanted low tariffs to allow cheaper imports of manufactured goods. Most manufacturers wanted high tariffs to protect their domestic market from foreign competition. Increasingly severe recessions and depressions caused American business leaders to fear that their domestic market had been saturated and that further growth could come only through exports. Many therefore demanded what they called an "open door" abroad for U.S. products: a dismantling of "protectionist" barriers that foreign countries put up to U.S. products. As the U.S. Department of State put it in 1898, "It is frequently asserted...that the output of factories working at full capacity is much greater than the domestic market can possibly consume, and it seems to be conceded that every year we shall be confronted with an increasing surplus of manufactured goods for sale in foreign markets if American operatives and artisans are to be kept employed the year round. The enlargement of foreign consumption of the products of our mills and workshops has, therefore, become a serious problem of statesmanship as well as of commerce."[7]

The language of free trade and protectionism would re-emerge in a very different context in the era of globalization.

Countering Downward Spirals

Despite their enormous growth, capitalist economies were marked by a chronic inability to fully utilize human and material resources—manifested in underemployed underclasses, mass unemployment, stagnation, recession, and depression.[8] Once they stopped growing, capitalist economies tended to enter a downward spiral in which worsening unemployment led to wage cuts which led to reduced demand for products which in turn led to still more unemployment, wage cuts, and reduction of demand. Human and material resources could lie unused even though people desperately need what they could produce.

Countering these downward spirals became a central political concern. To assure or restore growth, national governments created various kinds of non-market structures. Nineteenth century banking crises led to the development of central banks like the U.S. Federal Reserve Board to control money and credit. The Great Depression of the 1930s led to "Keynesian" policies— named after British economist John Maynard Keynes.

Keynes argued that lack of economic growth was the result of inadequate economic demand: unemployed or low-paid workers couldn't buy back all that the economy could produce. Keynesian policies stimulated economic demand by encouraging higher wages, government spending, expanded credit, and "welfare state" programs. This expanded government economic role helped stabilize the economy; it also strengthened the sense of a shared national economic interest and provided ordinary citizens a greater stake in the national economy.

Underlying shared national economic interest was the idea—first publicized by Henry Ford—that high wages created a mass consumer market that was good for business as well as for workers because well-paid workers could buy the products they produced.

In the United States, this approach was spearheaded by a cluster of social experiments known as the New Deal,[9] whose wide-ranging programs were designed primarily to counter various aspects of the Great Depression's downward spiral. These programs included public employment (Works Progress Administration and Civilian Conservation Corps); farm price supports (Agricultural Adjustment Act); environmental restoration (reforestation and land conservation); labor rights (Wagner Act); minimum wages and standards (National Recovery Act and Fair Labor Standards Act); cooperative enterprises (Works Progress Administration support for self-help); public infrastructure development (TVA and rural electrification); subsidized basic necessities (food commodity programs and Federal Housing Act); construction of schools, parks, and housing (Civil Works Administration); and income maintenance (Social Security Act).

Besides its famous "alphabet soup" of Federal government agencies, the New Deal was part of a process of social change that included experimentation at a state, regional, and local level; organization among labor, unemployed, urban, the elderly, and other grassroots constituencies; and lively debate on future alternatives that went far beyond the policies actually implemented.

Regulated Capitalism

As is often pointed out, the New Deal didn't cure the Great Depression. Only "government intervention" on a vastly larger scale—namely, World War II—did that. But the policies of the New Deal became the basis for the era of nationally regulated capitalism that followed World War II, providing the groundwork for the longest period of sustained growth in the history of capitalism. By one path or another, all the major capitalist countries came to a similar pattern of capitalism regulated by the nation state.

Keynesian policies were initially supported by coalitions that included labor and other popular movements and growth-oriented capitalists. By the end of World War II, "fiscal and monetary policy"—government spending and credit to regulate economic growth—were standard policy in all capitalist countries.[10] When unemployment rose, governments of all political complexions stimulated their economies by increasing government spending, cutting taxes, and lowering interest rates.

The quarter century that followed World War II was the heyday of what has been called "regulated capitalism."[11] The years from 1948 to 1973 saw a global growth rate of nearly 5 percent per year, with a moderation of booms and busts most unusual in the history of capitalism.

Regulated capitalism was supported in the most industrialized countries by a sort of class truce. After the intense class conflict of the late 1930s and early 1940s, a large part of U.S. business accepted the need to deal with workers organized in their own unions. The labor movement became institutionalized within firms, industries, communities, and the political system. Full employment and union seniority systems provided considerable job security. While traditional victims of discrimination, notably women and people of color, did not share equally in the benefits of this system, living conditions for most people improved substantially. The dominant wings within both the major political parties accepted this system of regulated capitalism and strove to perfect, not to transform it. Social movements increasingly looked to national governments for the solution to social problems.

Regulated capitalism left many of the longstanding problems of capitalism—such as the unequal distribution of wealth and power, the system's drive for unlimited growth, its destructiveness toward the environment, and its unresponsiveness to many non-market needs and purposes—intact. But it did have a major impact on unemployment and economic growth.

The Bretton Woods System

In the wake of World War II, the victorious powers feared an unregulated world market would mean a return to world depression, mass impoverishment, popular radicalism, Communism, and perhaps world war. They therefore entered into the Bretton Woods Agreement, which established institutions to regulate the international economy. This "Bretton Woods System" was based on U.S. global hegemony—in 1950, the United States provided 40 percent of the world's production and possessed military, political, and, some even believed, moral power to match.

The Bretton Woods Agreement created an IMF, which supported fixed exchange rates among different national currencies. It also established a World Bank to aid reconstruction and development. John Maynard Keynes, the chief British delegate, urged the creation of a world central bank to regulate global growth. The United States instead insisted that the U.S. dollar be the reserve currency for the whole system, letting the U.S. Treasury function as a world central bank, printing money as it saw fit.

Policy planners in the U.S. Treasury Department envisioned a post-war "free trade" system organized through an International Trade Organization. But the U.S. Congress insisted on partial protection of U.S. markets and scuttled the International Trade Organization. So the principal trading nations turned to another organization, the GATT. GATT was a system of agreements which created rules for a world market based on the "most favored nation" (MFN) principle, according to which nations agree to give each other trade conditions as favorable as those they give to any other nation. A series of negotiations—the "Tokyo Round," the "Kennedy Round" and others—substantially reduced tariffs by mutual agreement among GATT's scores of members.

For the quarter century after their founding, the IMF, World Bank, and GATT were quite successful in their technical missions, but they remained weak and subordinate in relation to nation states. They served as an adjunct rather than an alternative to nation-based capitalism. In the era of globalization, however, they were to become the nuclei around which a system of global economic governance would begin to form.

Chapter
Three

The Dynamics of
Globalization

Why did the system of nationally regulated capitalism give way to globalization and the New World Economy with their downward leveling and race to the bottom? The answer lies in large part in the strategies corporations developed to meet a crisis in the system of nationally regulated capitalism.

The Crisis of Nationally Regulated Capitalism

Regulated capitalism and the Bretton Woods system contributed to the unprecedented period of sustained growth in the world capitalist economy from World War II to the early 1970s. But in the early 1970s capitalism entered a worldwide crisis. Global economic growth fell to 2.5 percent, half its former rate. Profit rates in the seven richest industrialized countries fell from 17 percent in 1965 to 11 percent in 1980; for manufacturing they fell from 25 percent to 12 percent.[1] A wide range of expectations, based on the assumption that post-war growth rates would continue, were not fulfilled. As Peter Peterson noted in 1987, "The awkward but enduring fact is that, taken together, the claims of our various national interests and global obligations will far outrun our available resources to sustain or defend them."[2]

The end of the era of post-war growth and the beginning of the era of protracted crisis was marked by the U.S. decision in 1973 to renounce the Bretton Woods system of fixed exchange rates. Economists are still debating the causes of this crisis. In part it can be understood as one more example of the periodic downward spirals that have marked capitalism from its inception. It also reflects major changes among national economies: as war-devastated Europe and Japan revived and over a hundred former European colonies became politically independent nations, international competition intensified and the United States lost its dominant position as "global hegemon."[3] Heavy military spending, while increasing short-term demand, provided a long-term drain on productive investment; the Vietnam war in particular weakened the U.S. economy.

The Third World Alternative

One possible approach to global change was to update the system of national and global regulation. In response to the increasingly chaotic global economy of the 1970s, the Third World governments of the South attempted to initiate such an alternative. Working through the United Nations Conference on Trade and Development (UNCTAD), they called for a "North-South Dialogue" to develop a "New International Economic Order" (NIEO). In place of domination by Northern interests, they called for the regulation of global market forces in the interest of the development process. They advocated price and production policies and long-term sales agreements designed to stabilize the prices of the commodities they produced. They did not propose to replace capitalism, but they did insist that the world economy be managed to support the development and relative self-reliance of poorer countries.

In several rounds of North/South negotiations, the wealthy nations of the North showed some willingness to discuss such new arrangements. These discussions culminated in 1981 at a meeting of 22 heads of government in Cancun, Mexico, where, as Chairman of the South Commission Julius Nyerere recalls, "Reagan said 'no' and that was it. What was very revealing, and very depressing, was that after Reagan said 'no,' the other leaders from the North said that was the end."[4]

The New Corporate Strategies

Corporations experienced the economic crisis that began in the early 1970s as an intensification of international competition and a fall in their profits. As Jacques de Larosiere, chairman of the IMF, put it in 1984, there was a clear pattern of "substantial and progressive long term decline in rates of return to capital." Corporations increasingly saw the system of national economic regulation and class compromise as a barrier to increasing their profits. The solution increasingly came to be seen as cutting labor and other costs. As de Larosiere delicately put it, there was a need for "a gradual reduction in the rate of increase in real wages over the medium term if we are to restore adequate investment incentives."[5]

Faced with intensifying international competition, corporations began experimenting with strategies to increase their profits by reducing their labor and other costs. These strategies included moving their operations to lower-cost locations; transforming their own structures to operate in a highly competitive global economy; challenging national policies that increased their costs; and creating a new system of global economic governance which supported their other strategies. In short, they initiated the race to the bottom whose results we saw in Chapter One.

• Capital Mobility

At the core of the new strategy was *capital mobility*—the ability to move capital around the world. New transportation, communication, and production technology helped make this possible, but the process was largely driven by a wish to lower production costs. As economist David Ranney writes, "There is a strong interconnection between capital mobility and the cheapening of the costs of production." Mobility offers the opportunity "to move to low cost areas" and "pit the peoples of different nations against one another." By using the threat of moving as a club, "corporations can extract wage and work rule concessions from workers in their home country." And mobility allows companies to challenge or escape such claims on value as "health care, welfare, and subsidized housing programs; worker and consumer safety standards; and environmental regulations."[6]

The new capital mobility first became highly visible when First World corporations began to move production "off-shore"—primarily to "export processing zones" (EPZs) in Third World countries. These were generally in military dictatorships and authoritarian "development states" with little pretense of democracy. Some of these countries, notably the "Asian Tigers" like Korea, parlayed their cheap labor and repressive social control into rapid economic growth, becoming known as the "Newly Industrialized Countries" (NICs). East, South, and Southeast Asian countries experienced annual growth rates up to 37 percent between 1985 and 1989; Southeast Asia alone received 48 percent of all foreign direct investment going to developing countries.[7] The strategy of combining domestic repression with production for the new global economy spread from the original Tigers to many other countries, now including communist Vietnam and China. Indeed, "off-shore production" turned out to be just the first stage of a far more universal process of globalization.

The mobility of capital was enormously amplified by the development of global capital markets. In 1978, *Business Week* noted that large corporations were creating a demand for "stateless money."[8] Appearing first as "Eurodollars," such "stateless money" turned out to be the leading edge of a globalization of finance. As financier Felix Rohaytyn observes, "Despite the threats and conflicts within different regions, one development has gone ahead relentlessly throughout the world: the growth of global capital markets. A genuine worldwide market in stocks, bonds, currencies, and other financial instruments has emerged, tied together by modern data-processing and communications technology, and operating twenty-four hours a day, seven days a week...The total investment in the financial markets in the developing countries—including for example Mexico, India, and China—is now $180 billion, up from $2.4 billion seven years earlier."[9] This explosive globalization of what used to be called the "paper economy" sucks funds out of productive activities into financial speculation and generates runs on banks, currencies, and stock and bond markets.

Capital mobility sharply limited the ability of national governments to pursue Keynesian growth policies. When one country pursued full employment, the result tended not to be expanded production but inflation and trade deficits. Jimmy Carter and Francois Mitterand both tried Keynesian growth strategies, but encountered inflation, trade deficits, and financial crises, and abandoned the attempt. In 1986, after five years of monetary restraint, Britain turned to economic stimulus, expecting strong economic growth. Steven Ratner of Lazard, Freres & Co. notes that, "When the British economy was stimulated, the result was not higher domestic output but higher imports and higher inflation"—inflation over 10 percent a year. Economic stimulation in a single country backfired, whoever attempted it.[10]

• Restructuring the Corporation

The large, vertically integrated mass production firms that had dominated the world's markets for most of the 20th century staggered in the face of the global economic crisis. They were frequently portrayed as dinosaurs, doomed to die out in competition with small, nimble competitors. But a recent study by economist Bennett Harrison provides a very different and far more credible interpretation of corporate restructuring.

According to Harrison, the "signal economic experience of our era" is not "an explosion of individual entrepreneurship" but rather "the creation by managers of boundary-spanning networks of firms, linking together big and small companies operating in different industries, regions, and even countries."[11] Big firms "create all manner of networks, alliances, short- and long-term financial and technology deals—with one another, with governments at all levels, and with legions of generally (although not invariably) smaller firms who act as their suppliers and subcontractors." But the locus of ultimate power and control "remains concentrated within the largest institutions: multinational corporations, key government agencies, big banks and fiduciaries, research hospitals, and the major universities with close ties to business." Harrison describes this "emerging paradigm of networked production" *as concentration of control combined with decentralization of production.*[12] Businesses which are unable or unwilling to globalize are at a great disadvantage, since "The more the economy is globalized, the more it is accessible only to companies with a global reach."[13]

Harrison describes four building blocks of the emerging managerial paradigm. First, corporations pursue "lean production" by downsizing in-house operations to "core competences," farming out other work to "rings" of outside suppliers. Second, they use computerized manufacturing and management information systems to coordinate their far-flung activities across organizational and national borders. Third, "the most successful big firms have been busily constructing so-called strategic alliances among one another, both within and, especially, across national borders." Fourth, managers attempt to elicit "active collaboration of their most expensive-to-replace workers in the 'mission' of the corporation" through various kinds of worker participation.[14] "Lean production, downsizing, outsourcing, and the growing importance of spatially extensive production networks governed by powerful core firms and their strategic allies, here and abroad, are all part of businesses' search for 'flexibility,' in order to better cope with heightened global competition."[15]

According to Harrison, these "restructuring experiments" are "polarizing the population" and contributing to "growing inequality." The reason is that they create "sectors of low-wage, 'contingent' workers, frequently housed within small business suppliers and subcontractors. The advent of these generally big firm-led core-ring production networks is almost surely adding to the national (and increasingly international) problem of 'working poverty,' in which people work for a living but do not earn a living wage."[16]

• National Policies

Large corporations once had promoted nationally regulated capitalism, but in the context of deepening crisis they began to see it as an obstacle to their emerging strategies. Corporate leaders and the think tanks and economists associated with them evolved a new public policy agenda designed to overcome this obstacle. This Corporate Agenda appeared under a variety of labels, including monetarism, deregulation, laissez-faire, neo-liberalism, and supply-side economics.[17]

Economic policymakers deliberately encouraged downward leveling.[18] They used high unemployment to fight inflation. They cut wages, public services, and environmental protection to reduce businesses' production costs. Unemployment and falling real wages led to declining consumer demand for products worldwide, and policymakers no longer tried to counter this effect with Keynesian policies. The "class compromise" which had given labor and other non-elite groups a voice in the economic policies of many countries was renounced, and unions and other popular forces were marginalized in the political process and in some countries repressed.

Those whose voices were allowed to be heard in policy debates formed a dominant consensus around a simple but dubious formula: Each country should reduce costs for labor and government in order to become "more competitive" in the global economy. All will benefit because goods and services will be provided by those whose "comparative advantage" enables them to produce more cheaply.

In the United States, a political base for the Corporate Agenda was created by means of an alliance, consummated within the Republican Party, between large corporations and right-wing, formerly fringe elements expressing racial, gender, and religious resentment against the social changes of the 1960s and 1970s.[19] While the Corporate Agenda was already affecting public policy in the last two years of the Carter Administration, it began to be fully implemented with the election in 1980 of Ronald Reagan.

- International Institutions

As the economic crisis deepened, there gradually evolved what David Ranney has called a "supra-national policy arena" which included new organizations like the Group of Seven industrial nations (G-7) and NAFTA and new roles for established international organizations like the EU, IMF, World Bank, and GATT.[20]

The policies adopted by these international institutions allowed corporations to lower their costs in several ways. They reduced consumer, environmental, health, labor, and other standards. They reduced business taxes. They facilitated the move to lower wage areas and the threat of such movement. And they encouraged the expansion of markets and the "economies of scale" provided by larger-scale production.

The IMF and World Bank. The Bretton Woods Agreement established the World Bank to help rebuild Europe and the IMF to maintain fixed exchange rates for currencies, but over time their functions changed radically. Starting in the 1950s, the World Bank became a major funder of development projects in the Third World. After 1972, fixed exchange rates were abolished, but the IMF took on much of the management of the exploding international debt crisis. As the debt of Third World countries soared, the IMF and World Bank began to require debtor countries to accept structural adjustment programs as conditions for new loans. These conditions "neatly coincide with the agenda of mobile capital and the cheapening of the costs of production"[21] for global corporations by:

> • radically reducing government spending, in order to control inflation and reduce the demand for capital inflows

from abroad, a measure that in practice translated into cutting spending in health, education, and welfare;

• cutting wages or severely constraining their rise to reduce inflation and make exports more competitive;

• liberalizing imports to make local industry more efficient and instituting incentives for producing for export markets, which were seen both as a source of much-needed foreign exchange and as a more dynamic source of growth than the domestic market;

• removing restrictions on foreign investment in industry and financial services to make the local production of goods and delivery of services more efficient, owing to the presence of foreign competition;

• devaluing the local currency relative to hard currencies like the dollar in order to make exports more competitive; and

• privatizing state enterprises and embarking on radical deregulation in order to promote allocation of resources by the market instead of by government decree.[22]

Most Third World governments abandoned the pursuit of a more just international economic order and instead acceded to virtually any conditions in exchange for loan renewals.[23] Their austerity plans in turn reduced markets for industrial products from developed countries. Similar "shock therapy" plans were imposed on the ex-communist countries as a precondition for loans and investment.

In 1994, a group of international bankers, former top financial officials, and monetary experts from the world's richest countries, headed by former U.S. Federal Reserve Board Chairman Paul Volcker, circulated a proposal to give the IMF "a central role in coordinating economic policies and in developing and implementing monetary reforms."[24] They argued that "there has been no reliable long-term global approach to coordinating policy, stabilizing market expectations, and preventing extreme volitility and misalignments among key currencies." They proposed several immediate measures, to be followed by "a more formal system for managing exchange rates." According to Kenneth H. Bacon of the *Wall Street Journal*, "The Volcker commission's plan would, in effect, require countries to relinquish some of their economic sovereignty."[25] Powerful interests began lining up both in support and in opposition to the plan.

The World Trade Organization. GATT was formed in 1948. In various rounds of negotiations, it established rules governing tariffs, quotas, and other measures that countries use to protect a particular industry or sector. Early in 1994, more than 100 member countries, accounting for four-fifths of world trade, signed an agreement to transform GATT into a World Trade Organization (WTO). If ratified by their governments, this agreement will create a powerful center of global economic governance.

The WTO is the product of GATT's "Uruguay Round," which began in Punte del Este, Uruguay in 1986. The United States put forward proposals to radically expand GATT's mission and power, in effect making it a vehicle for global enforcement of the Corporate Agenda. The expanded GATT program would preempt democratic self-government at local, national, regional, and global levels by defining such matters as environmental and consumer protection, labor law, worker health and safety protection, food security policies, national industrial planning, plant closing legislation, and restrictions on foreign ownership of industries as "non-tariff barriers to trade." It redefines "free trade" to mean the right of companies to go wherever they want and do whatever they want with as little interference as possible from anyone. Such "freedom" for corporations means restricting the freedom of governments and citizens. The WTO represents, in effect, a daring global *coup d'etat*.

GATT in many ways offered an ideal vehicle to implement the Corporate Agenda. It was dominated by the major trading countries, who often cut deals in private "green room" caucuses and then imposed them on a "take-it-or-leave-it" basis. It was not officially part of the United Nations and therefore was insulated from pressures that might be brought to bear by the poorer but more numerous countries of the South. Its activities were conducted largely in secret. Its mission was restricted to reducing "barriers to trade." And it wielded the powerful weapon of trade sanctions to enforce its decisions.

The WTO involves a transformation of GATT's governance structure. While GATT was a contract among countries whose rules any country could veto or opt out of, the WTO will be a "legal personality" like the United Nations or World Bank. Its rules will be binding on all members.

At the core of WTO power will be "dispute resolution panels." Any WTO member country can challenge the domestic laws of any other member as violations of WTO rules. The charges will be heard before secret panels of three "trade experts" with no right of citizens or their organizations to testify or even to observe. A panel's decision will be automatically adopted within a fixed number of days unless *every* WTO member—including the initial complainant—votes to reverse it. If a country's laws are found to violate WTO rules, the laws must be eliminated. If they aren't, trade sanctions will be imposed automatically unless *every* member country votes against them. The trade panels will in effect have dictatorial powers over governments. (In May, 1994 the European Union circulated a list of the U.S. laws it wanted to challenge under the WTO, which included the Marine Mammal Protection Act, the Nuclear Non-Proliferation Act, food safety laws, California's Safe Drinking Water and Toxic Enforcement Act, and many others.)

The range of economic activity covered will also be enormously expanded. While GATT has primarily regulated trade in goods, WTO rules will cover agriculture, services, investment, and "intellectual property rights." They will apply to state and local governments—and any state or local law will be subject to challenge if it is more restrictive than national law. The WTO will establish ceilings for environmental, food, and safety standards; national standards will be subject to challenge if they are higher than the WTO standards—but, incredibly enough, not if they are lower.

The WTO will also intensify the gap between global rich and poor. According to an OECD/World Bank study, the industrialized countries will receive 70 percent of the additional income resulting from increased trade; at the opposite pole, Africa by 2002 will lose $2.6 billion.[26] "Free trade" rhetoric notwithstanding, little was done to open developed country markets to developing country products. The WTO can be expected to work hand-in-hand with the IMF and World Bank to impose the Corporate Agenda on developing countries.

The treaty establishing the WTO, while portrayed as a vehicle for eliminating regulation, runs to more than 22,000 pages and weighs 395 pounds.[27] As Ralph Nader put it, these texts "formalize a world economic government dominated by giant corporations, without a correlative democratic rule of law to hold this economic government accountable."[28]

Regional Institutions. The era of globalization has also seen a proliferation of regional "free trade" agreements and institutions. These institutions generally incorporate large elements of the Corporate Agenda. At the same time, they have the potential to serve as regional blocs should the global economy break down into hostile, competing regions.

In the wake of World War II, the countries of Western Europe created institutions for regional economic and political cooperation which eventually evolved from the European Economic Community (EEC) to the European Community (EC) to the European Union (EU). Their goals included preserving peace and democracy as well as reducing barriers to trade.

The EU represents a so-far unique experiment in transnational governance whose future direction remains unclear. In the era of regulated capitalism, the EU took on many of the regulatory functions of a government. It provided extensive support for economic development in poorer regions and initiated a "social charter"—not accepted by the United Kingdom—to protect labor and other rights and standards. In response to the emerging Corporate Agenda, however, the EU has increasingly become a vehicle for forcing national governments to admit all imports that meet EU standards, even if they don't meet higher national standards.

In 1990, U.S. President George Bush and Mexican President Carlos Salinas decided to launch negotiations for a Mexican-U.S. Free Trade Agreement. The initiative came from the Mexican elite, which had unsuccessfully sought help from Europe in meeting their deep economic crisis and finally had turned reluctantly to the United States. Canada, fearing exclusion from the proposed free trade zone, asked to join the negotiations for what was thereafter dubbed the North American Free Trade Agreement.

The Corporate Agenda had already been affecting economic relations between the United States and Mexico. Over the course of the 1980s, Mexico had cut its tariffs from 100 percent or more to less than 10 percent, and over 1,700 U.S. (and a growing number of Japanese) companies had established plants employing nearly half-a-million workers in Mexican free trade zones known as "maquiladoras." NAFTA's 2,000 pages of details represented in large part a "wish list" eliminating inconveniences faced by U.S. businesses that wanted to operate in Mexico. Despite massive opposition in the United States and Canada and more veiled criticism in Mexico, NAFTA went into effect January 1, 1994. Other countries, notably Chile, may enter negotiations to join the agreement.

Other regional trade institutions are proliferating. Asia has the Association of Southeast Asian Nations (ASEAN) and the Bangkok Agreement. The Pacific has the Asia Pacific Economic Cooperation (APEC). Latin America has the Central American Common Market (CACM), the Andean Common Market (ANCOM), the Southern Cone Common Market (MERCOSUR), and several others. Europe, Africa, the Middle East, and Oceania provide at least a dozen more. These organizations, which generally operate in accordance with the rules of GATT, are creating what has been called "layered governance" in the global economy.[29]

The New Global Governance

Globalization is bringing out some of the contradictions that have marked the nation-state system from its beginnings. Even the regulated democratic national welfare state never adequately addressed the inherent unreality of absolute state sovereignty and independence. Nationalist theories notwithstanding, the world was not made up of distinct peoples living in contiguous territories; more powerful states dominated less powerful ones; the world was too interdependent for even powerful states to truly determine what happened within the territories they governed; markets and businesses operated internationally and did not necessarily have the same interests as "their" states and peoples.[30] The concept of absolute national sovereignty, which continues to be the basis of most international law, regularly comes into conflict with such principles as universal human rights and the obligations of states under the UN Charter.

National governments have ceded much of their power to a "New Institutional Trinity"[31]—the IMF, World Bank, and GATT/WTO. These agencies increasingly set the rules within which individual nations must operate, and they increasingly cooperate in pursuit of the same objectives—objectives generally indistinguishable from the Corporate Agenda.

Rather than eliminate national governments, this new system of global economic governance adds another institutional layer—one that will at times conflict with national governments and may sometimes have to bow to them. It lacks the police and military organizations for dominion at home and war abroad that have characterized states from their origin. But its ability to impose its rules on its subordinate parts has nonetheless proved increasingly effective.[32]

Just as the states of early modern Europe often served and were supported by the emerging class of capitalists, this new system of global economic governance serves and is supported by the emerging global corporations. Like the absolute monarchs of yore, the IMF, World Bank, and GATT/WTO have little formal accountability to anyone except themselves, but they understand that in reality their power derives from their alliance with a powerful class. The functions they perform are more limited than those of conventional governments—limited to the functions that accord with the Corporate Agenda. Just as the absolute monarchs defined themselves as performing God's will on earth, so the new system of economic governance defines itself as a tool carrying out the work of the "invisible hand" of the market.

Like the absolutist states of the past, this new system of global governance is not based on the consent of the governed. It has no institutional mechanism to hold it accountable to those its decisions affect. No doubt for this reason, it also fails to perform those functions of modern governments that benefit ordinary people. It should come as no surprise that, like the monarchies of the past, this emerging system of undemocratic power is calling forth revolts.

Chapter
Four

The Flawed Debate

Although globalization has become a buzzword, discussion in the political arena and the media generally remains rooted in the paradigms of nation-based economies. In that era, the essential economic choices appeared to be between an active role for national governments versus "leaving it to free market forces." In the era of globalization, national economic policies are largely overwhelmed by the forces of global corporations, markets, and economic institutions. Yet arguments about "free trade," "protectionism, " and the like continue as if we were still dealing with a predominantly national economy.

The public debate at present has three great flaws. First, it fails to recognize the way globalization changes the very meaning of the words and concepts we use to describe the economy. Second, the labels and arguments used are often inadvertently or deliberately deceptive. Third, voices advocating "globalization-from-below" as an alternative to today's "globalization-from-above" are largely excluded from the debate.

This chapter tries to correct those flaws. It shows how globalization changes the meaning of concepts held over from the era of nation-based economies. It applies some truth-in-labeling to the ways these concepts are used now. And it distinguishes the new voice of globalization-from-below from both nationalism and corporate-oriented internationalism.

Free Trade

The terms of the public debate on international economics have been set primarily by those who portray themselves as advocates of "free trade." These advocates include the overwhelming majority of economists, business leaders, politicians, and experts of all kinds whose quotes and soundbites appear in the media. Their arguments have been crucial in justifying the New World Economy.

- ## Free Trade and Globalization

Free traders argue that removing barriers to trade reduces economic inefficiency and thereby benefits all. They generally base their argument on the classic economic doctrine of "comparative advantage." If each nation specializes in those activities in which it is most productive, total wealth will be increased. If Italy's climate is superior for producing wine and Jamaica's superior for producing sugar, both will be better off if they specialize where they have a "comparative advantage" and then trade the products. For Italy to try to produce sugar and Jamaica wine is simply inefficient and irrational.

This argument is used over and over to justify "free trade" agreements like NAFTA and GATT and to condemn government efforts to regulate trade. Yet it has become less and less relevant in the era of globalization.

As corporations have become global, goods and services are increasingly produced in "global networks" of large corporations and their dependent suppliers. The "United States" or "Japanese" computers that "U.S." or "Japanese" companies "trade" are actually produced in dozens of countries by corporate networks that include companies in both the countries that are supposedly "trading" with each other. If a "U.S." company contracts with producers in Japan, Indonesia, Columbia, and China to make and assemble an athletic shoe, which it then sells in 100 countries, who is trading with whom? It has become misleading to portray national economies as separate units that produce goods and services and then trade them with each other.

Even the doctrine of "comparative advantage" itself is growing less and less relevant. Fewer and fewer products are subject to much "comparative advantage" in the sense of an inherent advantage for one country: General Motors or Toyota can set up essentially the same car factory with virtually the same productivity in the United States, Mexico, or China. Of course, it is possible to consider cheap labor, poor environmental protections, and low social costs as "comparative advantages." But if the search for "comparative advantage" leads production to move where such "advantages" are greatest, the result is not the benefit of all but rather a race to the bottom.

• Free Trade or Freedom for Capital?

Classic free trade doctrine was about trade—goods and services produced in one country and exchanged for those from another. But a major part of the "trade debate"—and the bulk of the new "trade agreements" like NAFTA and GATT—are far less about reducing barriers to trade than about reducing barriers to the movement of *capital*. Yet freedom to move capital is constantly spoken of as a matter of freedom of "trade." In 1982, Harry J. Gray, then Chairman and CEO of United Technologies Corporation and one of the architects of the Corporate Agenda, gave a masterful example of this sleight-of-mouth. "We need conditions that are conducive to expanded trade," he argued. Then he non-sequitured to: "That means a worldwide business environment that's unfettered by government interference." GATT-ese accomplishes the same result by labelling regulations on investment as "Trade-Related Investment Measures" or "TRIMs. "[1]

Free traders generally wrap their arguments in the language of "free market" economics—the doctrine that all governmental and social practices which "interfere" with free market exchange should be reduced to a minimum. They argue in effect that public policy and social practice should aim to maximize the production and consumption of exchangeable goods and services. They call for eliminating government activity that interferes with the profit-maximizing dynamic of the market.

Today's free traders promote this view on a global basis. They call for a world economy in which all forms of public regulation of private economic enterprise are severely restricted or even banned. They define such matters as environmental protection, labor law, worker health and safety protection, food security policies, national industrial planning, plant closing legislation, and restrictions on foreign ownership of industries as "interference with free trade." Restrictions on such "interference" form a major part of so-called "trade agreements" like NAFTA and GATT.

- **Defending Free Trade**

Free traders follow three rather different approaches to reconciling their doctrine—rooted in the era of nation-based economies—with the realities of globalization.

One approach is simply to speak as if nothing has changed. For example, to support NAFTA and GATT the Clinton administration poured out reams of economic projections showing how much reductions in tariffs would increase U.S. trade, production, and jobs. They were largely silent about the thousands of pages in these agreements devoted to protecting capital mobility, limiting local, state, and national governments, and creating regional and global institutions of economic governance. The administration's constant theme has been "the United States can compete successfully in the global economy"—as if "the United States" were still an independent economic entity.

A second approach is not only to acknowledge but to celebrate the decline of the nation state and the rise of an unregulated New World Economy ruled mainly by markets. Walter Wriston, former chairman of Citicorp, compares the decisions made by currency traders at "200,000 monitors in trading rooms all over the world" to the democratic election of government officials. "Everyone is in control through a kind of global plebiscite on the monetary and fiscal policies of the governments." He acknowledges that, "Even though Americans have accepted the ballot box as the arbiter of who holds office, this new global vote on a nation's fiscal and monetary policies is profoundly disturbing to many." But Wriston sees the replacement of "the power and privilege of sovereignty" with market-based "discipline on the economic policies of imprudent governments" as positive. "The new system punishes bad monetary and fiscal policies almost immediately."[2]

A third approach recognizes that a market needs rules and that a global economy in fact requires global governance. It therefore supports an activist role for institutions like the IMF, World Bank, and GATT. But it deceptively wraps this activist role under the label of "free trade." Much of what is advocated as "free trade" is in fact nothing but a false labeling of the Corporate Agenda—the establishment of global rules and governance structures, albeit totally anti-democratic ones.

- ### The Downsides of Free Trade

"Free trade" in its various applications has contributed mightily to the "seven danger signals" described in Chapter One. It opens the starting gate to the race to the bottom. It dismantles the non-market structures that could counter the downward spiral. It countermands efforts to correct the polarization of rich and poor. It sanctifies the erosion of democratic governance. It argues for multifaceted "freedom" for global corporations. It legitimates unaccountable global institutions like the IMF, World Bank, and GATT as merely vehicles for enforcing "free trade." It promotes an uncontrolled economy which provokes its victims to see extremist nationalism as the only alternative.

Even in terms of the advantages usually claimed for it, a global free market is a questionable system. While in the short-term deregulation may increase competition, the long-term effect may well be to increase monopoly. Already, global deregulation under the banner of "free trade" is producing transnational mergers, joint ventures, and collusive arrangements between customers and suppliers, suggesting an emerging pattern of cartelization. No global anti-trust policy forestalls such a development.

Nor is the evidence clear that a global free market actually supports economic growth. Worldwide economic growth averaged almost 5 percent per year in the era of "regulated capitalism" from 1948 to 1973. In the following fifteen years it averaged only half that—despite the revolution in technology and the globalization of the economy. In the years after 1989 global growth slowed to a trickle.

When public policy and social practice seek solely to maximize private profit in the market, they slight other values of great significance. These include:

- democratic decisionmaking

- environmental protection

- social caring

- equality

- human solidarity

- community stability

- individual and family security

- long-term public and private planning and investment

- dignity in the work process

- goods and services consumed collectively

- cultural diversity

Surely these are among the "broad human interests" that an economic system should seek to sustain.

Nationalism

If "free traders" advocate a global free market, "economic nationalists" advocate using the power of national government to strengthen the national economy in its competition with other national economies.[3] Ways to do so range from activist trade policies to public investment to war.

• Activist Trade Policies

For hundreds of years, governments have found ways to favor "their" producers against "foreign" ones. These include tariffs, import quotas, regulations, subsidies, and informal barriers of many kinds. Sometimes these methods are used to aid particular products or industries; other times they function across-the-board. While "free traders" rail against such measures as "protectionism," today every country engages in such protection to some degree.

The impact of globalization is often experienced as a threat of "foreign competition. " Economic nationalists often seek to use national trade policies to improve conditions for "domestic" producers relative to foreign ones. Tariffs, quotas, and similar measures are often the response to a flood of imports.

Economic nationalists also often focus on other countries' trade policies, complaining that they discriminate against imports. For much of the 20th century, this orientation led the United States to demand that other countries provide an "open door" for U.S. products. Today this orientation is expressed in demands to "get tough on trade" and in the "Super-301" trade law which allows U.S. tariffs to be raised in retaliation against alleged discrimination against U.S. products. Such measures from time to time lead to "trade wars" in which each country raises its barriers higher in retaliation against similar protectionist measures by the other.

Such policies have become more and more problematic in the era of globalization. An "American" car is made of parts produced and assembled in dozens of countries; indeed, an "American" car may come off the same assembly line and include exactly the same parts as a "Japanese" car—except for the label. Furthermore, the global economy is now so integrated that nationalist policies are often self-defeating: when the United States threatened to raise tariffs on Japanese computer parts, for example, many U.S. companies howled that they would become "less competitive" if they couldn't buy the inexpensive Japanese components.

- **Increasing Competitiveness**

Nationalist critics of "free trade" point out that the countries that have been most successful in the globalizing economy do not follow free trade policies; much of their success is due to government economic initiative. These critics advocate increasing national competitiveness through such measures as industrial policy, managed trade, expanded educational programs, and new social and labor policies and work structures designed to give workers a stake in more flexible and productive employment and work practices. Their goal is to create a social and economic infrastructure that entices global corporations to keep or bring high-skill, high-wage employment. Many of the more progressive figures in the Clinton administration reflect this view.

While many of these proposals are worthy, "increasing national competitiveness" is not an adequate framework for addressing economic globalization because it does not grapple with the underlying problem of international capital mobility. If global corporations have no long-term interest in a given regime or country, they will resist paying the social overhead costs associated with strengthening the social and economic infrastructure. Further, if one country provides a good infrastructure but requires high wages, global corporations will still tend to move operations to other countries with good infrastructures but lower wages. Any economic strategy must come to terms with the fact that as long as global corporations can freely move their operations as they please, they can force any area to conform to their demands on threat of economic abandonment.

This nationalist approach falls into what could be called "the competitiveness trap." It defines the problem as a lack of national competitiveness, leading to the loss of jobs to foreign countries. It defines the solution as lowering costs of production so that companies will choose to produce in "our" country rather than elsewhere. It proposes to solve the problem by increasing productivity and lowering costs—ignoring the paradoxical effect of such efforts in aggravating the downward spiral.

- Militarism

Many though by no means all nationalists consider military force an acceptable means for pursuing national economic objectives. When Saddam Hussein invaded Kuwait, he justified it in terms of Kuwait's financial strangulation of Iraq. When George Bush organized Operation Desert Storm, he justified it as necessary to control access to oil and thereby preserve the "American way of life."

- The Politics of Nationalism

Of course, nationalism is more than a set of policies. It is a worldview, one often grounded in strong traditions and laden with deep emotions. It creates a group identity sharply distinguished from outsiders. It can easily lead to the mentality expressed by Russian nationalist Vladimir Zhirinovsky: "War is the natural state of man. Either they get us or we get them."[4]

Such a nationalist response has been very much part of the movements against downward leveling. In the United States, Ross Perot has repeatedly charged that at the core of U.S. economic difficulties lies the control of trade policy by foreign lobbyists and politicians influenced by them. At the height of the NAFTA debate he proposed a "social tariff" which would restrict the import of Mexican products until Mexican wages were closer to those of the United States—a restriction that would have been devastating to the Mexican workers for whom he professed such sympathy.

Nationalism is often articulated in the language of absolute sovereignty first developed to support European absolute monarchs. In the United States, some conservative politicians oppose the World Trade Organization negotiated in the Uruguay Round GATT agreement on the grounds that it will restrict U.S. sovereignty. Similar arguments were made against the EC and the Maastricht treaty in Europe, especially in the United Kingdom. In

Canada and Mexico, a call to protect national sovereignty played an important role in the struggle against NAFTA.[5]

Sovereignty often refers simply to self-government—the right of the members of a group or the residents of a territory to govern themselves. It represents the rejection of an imperialism in which one group or territory is ruled by another. But in nationalist ideology, sovereignty refers to the absolute right of the nation state to do whatever it wants to its own people or to others without "outside interference." It asserts that the nation state is the only proper vehicle for self-government, and that no interest should be higher than the national interest.

An exclusive focus on national interests distorts people's understandings of what is really going on in the global economy. During the 1980s, as U.S. manufacturers deliberately disinvested in U.S. industry and moved their operations "offshore," many U.S. workers directed their hostility to Japanese workers; "Toyota-bashing" became a highly publicized national sport. Corporations cannily exploited this attitude: at the very time it was abandoning steel plants instead of modernizing them, the U.S. Steel Corporation showed its workers a movie called "Where's Joe?" blaming job loss on Japanese competition and asking for protection against Japanese steel imports.

A purely national focus undermines efforts at transnational cooperation. For example, the idea of a common front by debt-stricken Third World countries in their negotiations with the creditor banks—dubbed a "debtor's cartel"—was widely discussed as a response to the debt crisis. In the end, however, the key countries backed down and cut individual—and highly disadvantageous— deals with the banks. As Brazilian Workers Party leader Luiz Inacio Lula da Silva—generally known as Lula—put it, every time a Latin American country tries alone to renegotiate better deals with Europe or the United States, "It's like placing a lightweight up against Mike Tyson—no matter how good he is, the odds are stacked against him and he ends up getting knocked out."[6]

An excessive focus on national sovereignty undermines efforts to impose better rules on the global economy. The same argument that would reject current GATT proposals as an interference with national sovereignty would rule out the inclusion of a corporate code of conduct or a social charter within such international institutions. The problem here goes beyond the economic sphere. An absolutist interpretation of national sovereignty undermines efforts to address such global problems as environmental destruction, nuclear proliferation, overpopulation, and human rights. Solutions to such problems require transnational forms of regulation that will limit national sovereignty, supported by a global civil society with identities and loyalties transcending the nation.

While love of country has evoked some of the highest expressions of devotion and self-sacrifice, and while it does not necessarily entail hostility to other peoples, the twentieth century has shown how easily nationalism can take destructive forms. From Nazi aggression to the drive for a "Greater Serbia" it has motivated and justified aggressive war. From the holocaust to "ethnic cleansing" and from recent U.S. "Mexico-bashing" and British "Paki-bashing" to German skinhead violence it has fomented ethnic, racial, and national hatred. From witchhunts against "un-Americans" to the blowing up of the Greenpeace ship *The Rainbow Warrior* by French intelligence officers, it has justified political repression.

The effects of downward leveling are easily exploited by nationalist and right-wing populist demagogues. Extreme nationalist and racist politicians in Russia rail against the impositions of the IMF. Eurofascists call for protection against "cheap foreign labor" from Eastern Europe and the Third World. A publication distributed in the United States during the struggle over NAFTA contained an article portraying NAFTA as a threat to U.S. workers and another denying the reality of the holocaust.

In the era of globalization, it is necessary to address our problem by means of global cooperation, not national competition. Even if we wish to move toward a less centralized economy with more national or local self-reliance, we need global rules and institutions to support the effort to do so.

Globalization-from-Below

Public discussion of the global economy is often conducted as if the issue were a continuation of the classic controversies of "free trade" vs. "protectionism" or "internationalism" vs. "nationalism." It is as if the only choices were the present form of globalization or a return to nation-based economies.

A new perspective, rooted in the realities of globalization, transcends these formulations. It might be called a democratic or people's internationalism or—as we will call it here—"globalization-from-below."

In contrast to nationalist approaches, globalization-from-below recognizes the need for transnational rules and institutions which may limit national sovereignty.

But globalization-from-below advocates far different functions for such institutions than do free traders or the Corporate Agenda. Globalization-from-below *opposes* global rules designed to force downward leveling, but supports global rules that, for example, protect labor and environmental rights and standards.

Globalization-from-below starts from the fundamental premise of democracy, that people should be able to make the decisions that affect their lives. It therefore argues—in sharp contrast to the Corporate Agenda—that global institutions must be democratic, transparent, accountable, and accessible to the public.

In many cases, the new international rules needed to block downward and promote upward leveling would greatly strengthen the ability of nations to govern themselves. For example, "globalization-from-below" alternatives to NAFTA and GATT have emphasized the right of countries to food security and the ending of World Bank and IMF dictation of national policies through structural adjustment programs.

In other cases, upward leveling requires international rules that empower people at the grassroots level—even if this limits aspects of national sovereignty. The movement for international labor rights, for example, advocates regulation at regional and global levels that would interfere with an absolutist definition of "national sovereignty" by requiring the meeting of certain minimum standards—but in a way that increases the ability of workers to organize themselves.[7]

Globalization-from-below, in contrast to today's globalization-from-above, does not imply a global centralization of power. As one advocate put it,

> One of the cornerstones of U.S. democracy was the practice of citizens working with public officials at local, state, and national levels to enact regulations and subsidies and incentives that protect the public welfare, health and safety, and environment...We are for new forms of internationalism, but forms which reinforce the right of localities, states, and nations to set their own high standards.[8]

Globalization-from-below implies not global centralization but rather a multilevel system of democratic governance. Globalization-from-below also rejects the effort of corporations to play non-elite groups in different countries off against each other. It sees the upward leveling of the conditions of those at the bottom as a common interest of all who are not in a position to exploit cheap labor, environmental, and social costs. The ability of people in each country to organize and raise their standards is beneficial to people in other countries.

Finally, globalization-from-below believes that, if corporations are going to cooperate worldwide to pursue their interests, ordinary people also need to do so. The advocates of globalization-from-below have put a strong emphasis on building cooperation among popular organizations and movements across national borders.

• Globalization-from-Below in the NAFTA Debate

The NAFTA debate saw for the first time the emergence of globalization-from-below perspectives in the U.S. political arena. Its advocates focused on the effects of capital mobility in fomenting a "race to the bottom." They encouraged upward leveling of labor and environmental conditions in Mexico. And they formed alliances with citizens' organizations in Mexico and Canada.

A broad anti-NAFTA coalition neither attacked Mexicans nor called for protection of U.S. markets against Mexican products. Rather, it emphasized the need to raise labor, social, and environmental conditions to prevent jobs from moving wherever such standards were lowest. It portrayed the issue not as a struggle of the U.S. versus Mexico but rather one of workers and citizens of both countries resisting a plan by corporations to play them off against each other.

Sections of this coalition went further. They engaged in extensive networking with citizen groups in Mexico and Canada. They organized active support for Mexican workers. And they engaged in a tri-national citizen's dialogue to produce an alternative to NAFTA called *A Just and Sustainable Trade and Development Initiative for North America*.

• **The Wider Context**

Like free trade doctrine, globalization-from-below recognizes the potential benefits of transnational economic ties. But like protectionism, it also recognizes their potential downsides. Like the Corporate Agenda, it recognizes the need for global rules to govern the global economy—but it advocates a very different set of rules and a different, more democratic way of making and implementing them. Like internationalism, it recognizes the need for global cooperation rather than economic war of nation against nation. But like nationalism, it sees present forms of globalization as a threat to democratic self-rule.

Economic globalization-from-below is part of a broad movement with implications far beyond the economic sphere. In the words of Richard Falk, globalization-from-below consists of "an array of transnational social forces animated by environmental concerns, human rights, hostility to patriarchy, and a vision of human community based on the unity of diverse cultures seeking an end to poverty, oppression, humiliation, and collective violence." Globalization-from-below is an expression of the spirit of "democracy without frontiers," mounting a challenge to "the homogenizing tendencies of globalization-from-above."[9]

Resistance Is Global

The triumph of globalization and the Corporate Agenda has generated an unanticipated and often unrecognized backlash. First, Second, and Third Worlds, North and South, developed and developing countries have all suffered the results of downward leveling, and this has generated popular pressures for change nearly everywhere. As Republican political analyst Kevin Phillips' *The American Political Report* notes, all over the world there is "a growing revulsion against conservative/market politics" with their "austerity, value-added taxes and entitlement cuts" designed to "keep financial markets and budgets safe for the economic elites." This is "a major new dimension" to what he calls "populist/radicalization politics" and, as he says, it is "hard to know where it'll end."[1]

First slowly, then with increasing speed, movements have emerged in many parts of the world to resist the effects of globalization. Their immediate goals have included saving jobs, restoring wage cuts, stopping toxic dumping, preserving small farms, subsidizing life necessities, redistributing land, blocking or revising trade agreements, winning labor rights, preventing privatization, preserving minimum wages and job security, and many others. Their tactics have included electoral politics, strikes and general strikes, civil disobedience and civil disturbances, marches, demonstrations, letter writing campaigns, legislative lobbying, and even armed uprisings.

These movements have often been marked by the formation of extraordinary coalitions. The struggle against NAFTA in the United States, for example, brought together the labor movement and a substantial part of the environmental movement—often antagonists in the past—as well as farm, consumer, and many other groups. The struggle against World Bank funding for destructive development of the Amazon rainforest brought together indigenous Amazonian rubber tappers, a global network of environmentalists, and native peoples throughout the Americas. Labor rights efforts have linked human rights advocates, trade unionists, and anti-poverty activists in First and Third Worlds.

These activities are without doubt responses to local conditions—but local conditions that are themselves in part the product of global forces. This resistance is developing within two superimposed but radically different spheres: the long-established nation-state system and the emerging global economy. This leads them to exhibit a continuing ambiguity—a peculiar intermixture of "left" and "right," "nationalist" and "internationalist" strands. The confusions of the flawed debate on the global economy affect the way these movements see their situation and define their goals.

Despite the links that have been made, this resistance is still highly fragmented. There are few if any direct connections between an uprising of indigenous people in Chiapas, a strike to preserve labor rights in Peoria, and student demonstrations against a reduced minimum wage in Paris. That fragmentation is easily exploited by those who would make different workforces, peoples, and communities compete with each other in the "race to the bottom."

This wave of resistance has received little recognition for several reasons. Global processes are often hard to recognize because our concepts stem from a world divided into nations, regional blocs, and First/Second/Third Worlds. The belief that globalization represents the wave of the future has led many to view resistance to it as simply pointless, retrograde, particularistic, and therefore without significance. The resistance is so fragmented that it is often easier to see the individual droplets than the wave. Yet looking back from a distance, it becomes evident that downward leveling has provoked a cascade of resistance in all parts of the world and in countries at all levels of development.

The first section of this chapter surveys various forms of resistance to globalization and the Corporate Agenda that have emerged in different parts of the world. The second section of this chapter focuses on the transnational movements that have developed in response to the growing power of the IMF, World Bank, GATT/WTO, and NAFTA. They show how the movement to resist globalization-from-above can itself become globalized.

A Global Survey of Resistance

• Third World Upheavals

As "structural adjustment programs" imposed by the IMF and World Bank squeezed the lifeblood out of poor countries and their poorer classes, so-called "IMF riots"—really mass upheavals and political crises—broke out in countries from Egypt to Brazil. In Venezuela in 1989, weeks of rioting were triggered when the government raised transport fares and other subsidized prices in response to IMF demands; 250 people were killed. In Morocco in 1990, a nationwide general strike demanded labor law reforms and a doubling of the minimum wage. According to a Reuters report, rioting broke out and "thousands of people rampaged through the streets, buildings were set afire, guests and staffers were plucked from a burning five-star hotel, and cars, buses, banks, and shops were attacked." Dozens of people were killed by rioters and troops. The report noted that "Hardships have been worsened by an austerity program introduced at the behest of the World Bank and the International Monetary Fund."[2] A few days after the upheaval, the government pledged to raise salaries and improve social benefits.

Strikes and general strikes have been a common form of Third World protest. In India in 1992, an estimated 15 million workers participated in a one-day nationwide industrial strike to protest the government's New Economic Policy (NEP). Unions maintained that the NEP was adopted under pressure from the IMF and World Bank as a condition for loans. They demanded a halt to privatization of public sector enterprises; an end to plant closures and labor retrenchment; a reduction in the prices of essential commodities; restrictions on the entry of foreign corporations; preservation of public sector banks; worker participation at all levels of management; and protection of the right to strike.[3] In Bolivia in 1994, after months of protests and social unrest, workers conducted a general strike, hunger strikes, and road and rail blockades. After 23 days of national work stoppage, the government agreed to a 15 percent raise in the minimum wage and other increases.[4]

People in the Third World have frequently used elections to express their opposition to the effects of globalization. In 1993, after five years of "structural adjustment" imposed by the IMF, Venezuelan voters threw out the parties that had run the country for 35 years and elected a president whose platform called for ending "free-market misery" by substituting a luxury tax for the value-added tax, ending privatization, restoring some state subsidies, protecting food production and the textile industry, and renegotiating the foreign debt.[5]

Most dramatic of all was the Chiapas uprising that began January 1, 1994, the date that NAFTA went into effect. Indigenous people organized as the Zapatista National Liberation Army seized the principal cities of the southern Mexican province of Chiapas, and triggered an unprecedented push for political and economic reform whose impact may well continue for years to come.

• Unionization in the NICs

As development-oriented dictatorships began transforming certain poor Third World countries into export processing zones, major revolts against authoritarian domination emerged in Korea, the Philippines, South Africa, Brazil, China, and other emerging or would-be NICs. From Soweto to Tiananmen Square, millions of people fought the political repression that undergirded the new economic domination.

At the heart of this resistance were often new labor movements organized in the new industries producing for the global economy. In South Korea in the 1980s, for example, "when the Korean state began to promote export-oriented industries, real wages began to stagnate, and relatively skilled workers began to use shop-floor strikes to demand higher pay and better working conditions... militant strikes were supported by working-class communities and student groups."[6] Korean wages went from 10 percent of the U.S. level in 1985 to 18 percent in 1988, principally due to "the upsurge of democratic and union rights which took place at the time."[7]

In Brazil, militant strikes began initially in the auto plants, whose workers launched a new labor federation that came to include textile, construction, transport, and agricultural workers. This new labor movement laid the basis for "a new class-based politics," insisting that "the demands of workers and their families be considered during the transition to civilian rule." In 1989, the former auto strike leader Lula da Silva came close to winning Brazil's first free presidential election in 20 years.[8]

In South Africa, "Workers in newly expanded heavy industries used shop-floor strikes, supported by consumer boycotts and community stay-aways, to push employers to negotiate with workers, as well as the state to reform labor legislation." South African union membership quadrupled from 700,000 in 1979 to 2.7 million in 1991—more than half of the non-agricultural workers.[9] The new union organizations "worked with community organizations to mobilize the uprising that spread across South Africa in the second half of the 1980s" and ultimately forced an end to apartheid.[10]

As Gay Seidman, author of a comparative study of labor movements in these NICs points out,

> In each case, workers responded to new organizational possibilities, using their position in new production processes

to mobilize pressure on employers and authoritarian regimes. Rather than concentrating only on improving the conditions of skilled workers, each labor movement included in their political agenda issues from outside the factory gates, issues reflecting the concerns of their wider communities...all three movements also challenged state control over workers' communities, articulating the demands of a broad working-class constituency.[11]

The New World Economy was in effect creating a new labor movement.

• The Ex-Second World

As the Berlin Wall came down and the Soviet Union dissolved, Western economists made plans for a rapid transition to a capitalist market economy. The IMF sent teams into each country to establish "shock therapy" programs similar to the structural adjustment programs imposed on the Third World.

The subsequent history of the formerly-communist countries has been one of economic disaster followed by mass rejection of free-market policies. On the eve of the Russian parliamentary election of December 1993, The Economist noted that 12 of the 13 parties contesting the elections called radical capitalist economic reform a failure.[12] In the election, parties ranging from ex-communists to neo-fascists trounced the advocates of "market reforms."

In 1993, "disheartened by the harsh aspect of capitalism at its ugliest," Poland, Slovakia, Lithuania, and Hungary voted opponents of shock therapy, including many former communist leaders, back into power.[13] In Poland, when the new government failed to keep its campaign promises to increase wages and spend more on welfare, 30,000 workers from all over Poland marched through Warsaw to protest.[14]

• First World Challenges

The mid-1990s saw a push by Western European governments and corporations to reduce established standards of work and life—and an explosion of resistance. Most highly publicized was the opposition to a French government plan to let employers pay young workers only 30 to 80 percent of the minimum wage. Hundreds of thousands of students and workers disrupted the major cities for weeks by disorderly demonstrations. Expressing fear of a rerun of the social upheaval of 1968, the government withdrew the plan.

In Spain, workers conducted a general strike to protest legislation to reduce unemployment benefits, freeze salaries of government workers, allow young workers to be paid less than the minimum wage, and make it easier for employers to fire their workers.[15] In Belgium, workers called a general strike, their first since 1936, to protest a government austerity package that froze real wages and cut welfare, health, and pension funds. The strike crippled transportation, shipping, postal service, and public schools and closed down the offices of such global corporations as GM, Bayer, and BASF.[16]

In the electoral arena, voters reacted against what *The American Political Report* referred to as "the 1980s excesses of capitalism." "In 1992, the Republican Party got its lowest share of the U.S. presidential vote in 80 years. In 1993, Canada's Progressive Conservatives got the worst drubbing ever given a Canadian government. In 1993, Japan's Liberal Democratic Party lost for the first time since 1955. In Britain, the conservative prime minister is setting records for low poll ratings, lost by-elections and party loss of local governments in England."[17] The gainers ranged from Greens to neo-fascists.

The Limits of National Resistance

These protests and rebellions indicate that the New World Economy does not have the consent of the world's people. Nor has dissent been without effect. A few weeks after the 1989 "IMF riots" in Venezuela, creditor countries announced the "Brady Plan" to write off part of Third World debt. Brazil, South Africa, and Korea have all won significant democratization and improvement in living standards. Some social benefits have been saved in Eastern Europe. The French minimum wage was preserved.

But the effectiveness of popular actions at a national level has been sharply limited by globalization. For example, in the first quarter after Venezuelan voters threw out the parties that had supported "structural adjustment," new foreign investment dropped by 30 percent and foreign reserves dropped by 17 percent. In response, the president—who as a candidate had advocated an end to "free-market misery"— declared, "We aspire to a free and competitive economy" and announced budget cuts, new taxes, and a radical privatization plan.[18] Similarly, the New Democratic Party, elected on an anti-NAFTA, anti-Corporate Agenda platform in Canada's richest and most populous province of Ontario, initiated what the Ontario Federation of Labour called "the most anti-worker intrusion into free collective bargaining in Canadian history," cancelling all public sector contracts and forcing $2 billion in concessions on union members.[19] In the United States, President Clinton quickly abandoned the public investment program on which he was elected in 1992— explicitly portraying his reversal as an effort to win approval from the bond market.[20] In Hungary, the former communist officials who won election in 1994 are expected to make little major change in economic policies. According to the director of Gallup Hungary, they "know there is a gap between what the voters want and what they can deliver. There are no easy solutions for them because they can't translate the anti-market, anti-privatization sentiment into reality."[21]

Resistance Globalized

One reason there appears to be no alternative to the New World Economy as it is currently developing is the difficulty of establishing *national* alternatives. But the globalization of corporations and economic institutions has begun to generate responses that cut across borders.

• World Bank/IMF Campaigns

Between 1968 and 1982, lending by the World Bank increased sixfold.[22] Its huge dam, road, forestry, agriculture, and other development projects, supposedly designed to help "the poorest of the poor," actually displaced millions of poor people and destroyed environments and traditional lifeways for millions more. During the 1980s, the Bank became the target for joint action by indigenous peoples, environmental and human rights activists in the affected Third World countries, and allies from the First World countries that funded the destructive projects. This cooperation has evolved into a coordinated challenge to the entire "structural adjustment" economic strategy that the World Bank and IMF are imposing throughout the Third World.

Saving the Amazon Rainforest. In the mid-1970s, the *seringueiros*—"rubber tappers"—who live in the Amazon rainforest and make their living by gathering sap from rubber trees began to resist the cutting down of the trees. They used what they called *"empate"*—stalemate—to protect their forest by peacefully standing in groups between the trees and the loggers who came to cut them down. A rubber tapper named Chico Mendes emerged as a prominent leader of these efforts.

Meanwhile, in 1983 U.S. environmental organizations persuaded Congress to hold hearings in which environmentalists, representatives of indigenous peoples, and anthropologists testified to the destruction of rainforests, contamination of rivers, and forced displacement of indigenous peoples caused by World Bank-funded projects, with the Amazon rainforest as a major case in point. The next year, environmental and human rights groups in Brazil began a joint research project with U.S. environmentalists and anthropologists to document the devastation caused by World Bank projects in the Amazon. Thirty-two nongovernmental organizations (NGOs) from eleven countries sent the results of this research to the World Bank with a demand for emergency measures to protect indigenous people and the environment. In response to pressures from NGOs and the U.S. Congress, the World Bank finally cut off the loan—the first time a public international financial institution had terminated a loan for environmental reasons.[23]

Cooperation among rubber tappers, indigenous peoples, Brazilian NGOs, and First World allies steadily deepened. In 1985, rubber tappers from all over the Amazon region met—with representatives of Brazilian and international NGOs present—and formed a National Council of Rubber Tappers. They called for the creation of "extractive reserves" to be preserved and sustainably harvested under the management of local rubber tapper communities. They formed an alliance with the Union of Indigenous Peoples called the Amazonian Alliance of the Peoples of the Forest. Over the next three years, Chico Mendes and representatives of indigenous, environmental, and human rights organizations travelled to the United States and lobbied the World Bank and the U.S. Congress. The World Bank was persuaded to endorse the rubber tappers' plan for extractive reserves. In 1988, Chico Mendes was murdered. But the plan for extractive reserves went forward: By 1992, the Brazilian government had created nineteen extractive reserves covering nearly three million hectares of rainforest.[24] The scandal of its role in destroying the Brazilian rainforests helped lead the World Bank to expand its environmental department and its involvement with environmental issues.

Fighting on a Global Plane. The cooperation to save the Amazon rainforest was a "novel form of international political action," but it was "only the best-known example of the newly formed global networks between local groups in developing countries and environmental activists and advocates in the North." Others included the Asia-Pacific Peoples Environmental Network, the World Rainforest Movement, and the International NGO Forum on Indonesia.[25] Starting in 1986, environmental, development, and human rights groups from around the world began holding counter-meetings—dubbed the International NGO Forum—at the annual joint meetings of the World Bank and IMF.[26]

The reach of this emerging network was extraordinary. In 1992, for example, when hundreds of thousands of rural people resisted the imminent destruction of their homes and livelihoods by the World Bank-funded Sardar Sarovar Dam in India's Narmada Valley, 900 NGOs from 37 countries threatened to initiate a campaign to cut off Bank funding unless it halted its support for the project. After repeated refusals to do so, in 1993 the Bank cancelled its loan for the project.

The quickest road to the Bank's heart was evidently through its funding. Prompted by environmental and human rights advocates, in 1993 the U.S. Congress cut its contribution to the Bank to press for more openness in the Bank's operations and the creation of an appeals panel to investigate citizen complaints. Canada and Finland made similar cuts.[27] "Unless the Bank does a better job of disclosing information about its lending practices, we'll just have to start cutting off the money" said U.S. Rep. Barney Frank, chairman of the House Banking Subcommittee on International Development.[28] The U.S. Congress also threatened not to fully fund a $12 billion capital increase for the IMF and passed legislation requiring the U.S. representative to the IMF to promote social, environmental, and human rights issues in its programs.

At the 1992 International NGO Forum, representatives from 46 countries launched a campaign to challenge the Structural Adjustment Programs of the World Bank and IMF. Said Horace Levy of the Social Action Center in Jamaica, "because the current recolonization process is global, we must fight it on a global plane."[29]

Organizations agreed to concentrate research on the global context and local-level impact of structural adjustment. They established an "NGO CASA" to disseminate this information. Regional action networks were established, such as the "Asian People's Solidarity Against Debt and Recolonization" created by NGOs from Bangladesh, Hong Kong, India, Indonesia, Japan, Malaysia, and the Philippines.[30]

These efforts came to a head in 1994 at the fiftieth anniversary of the World Bank and IMF, when NGOs all over the world organized a "Fifty Years Is Enough" campaign. The U.S. campaign, a coalition of over 100 environmental, development, religious, labor, and student organizations, called for cuts in U.S. contributions to the World Bank and IMF to force basic changes. Their platform included:

- full public accountability

- systematic integration of women and men affected by IMF and World Bank projects and policies into their formulation, implementation, monitoring, and evaluation

- a shift from environmentally destructive development to more self-reliant, resource-conserving development

- scaling down of Bank and IMF resources and the channeling of development funding through alternative institutions

- debt relief

Due in considerable part to the Campaign's work, the U.S. Congress in 1994 placed restrictions on funds for the World Bank and IMF until they improve disclosure, environment, and resettlement policies. Legislation requires the United States to condition its vote for loans on the requirement that borrowing countries "have and enforce laws affording internationally recognized worker rights" as defined by the ILO.[31]

Clearly these campaigns are far from strong enough to control such powerful global institutions as the World Bank and the IMF; it is remarkable that they have been able to influence their policies at all. Equally remarkable is the possibility they reveal for globally coordinated citizen action which unites a wide range of groups concerned with human rights, social justice, and the environment in North and South around common programs. If the World Bank and IMF are part of an emerging system of undemocratic, unaccountable global economic governance, perhaps the International NGO Forum and similar assemblies should be seen as the first germ cells of an emerging proto-parliament struggling to impose an increasing level of democratic accountability on these global institutions.

- ## Resisting the Free Trade Agreements

Starting in the mid-1980s, political leaders in the United States and elsewhere began a major effort to incorporate the Corporate Agenda in international trade agreements. As a result, GATT and NAFTA have been the focus of major political struggles in many countries. But despite the publicity these struggles have received, there has been little recognition that they are part of international movements involving people in dozens of countries. The campaigns against GATT and NAFTA are somewhat different from those against the World Bank and IMF in that less of their support comes from NGOs acting primarily out of concerns of conscience and more comes from popular organizations expressing the direct interests of their constituents. These campaigns against trade agreements give some sense of what it means to link large-scale popular action on a continental or even global basis.

GATT. The Uruguay Round of GATT negotiations that began in 1986 aimed to radically expand GATT to cover agriculture, services, investment, intellectual property, and "non-tariff barriers to trade." While its supporters claimed that the proposed agreement would benefit the entire world, many environmental, consumer, labor, farm, and other popular organizations in both the Third and the First World saw it as an effort by global corporations to ban all laws and regulations they disliked. These groups began a worldwide campaign that delayed completion of the Uruguay Round for several years and forced significant changes in its results.

Much of the initiative in exposing the significance of the GATT proposals came from a network of advocates for small farmers around the world. While the U.S. government had been promoting its trade proposals as beneficial for both U.S. and Third World agriculture, many critics argued that they would primarily benefit agribusiness and transnational commodity traders—and would drive millions of small farmers in both North and South off their farms.

Advocates for small farmers, who had gathered in Ottowa for an "international farm crisis summit" in 1983, continued to come together regularly through the 1980s for counter-meetings at the GATT negotiations. Said U.S. family farm advocate Mark Ritchie, a key initiator of international small-farm networking, "We learned to reverse the old slogan, 'Think globally, act locally.' We learned you have to act globally to succeed locally— you have to go to Brussels to save your farm in Texas. It was really important for farmers in different parts of the world to see their common circumstances and to develop win/win approaches, rather than being played off against each other."[32]

Dramatic mass actions by European farmers, combined with the farmers' political clout and wide public support, forced European governments to resist the U.S. GATT proposals. The farmers also began building transnational coalitions with other groups. Consumer, environmental, and farm groups from the United States, Japan, and Western and Eastern Europe, for example, met in Stuttgart and resolved to oppose GATT proposals that would "take the power to set health and safety standards away from elected leaders."

In the United States, a Fair Trade Campaign initiated by family farm groups brought together environmental, consumer, farm, and some labor organizations to challenge the U.S. GATT proposals. It focused on mobilizing grassroots political pressure to improve or block the proposed agreement.

Inside the Washington, D.C. Beltway, environmental groups like Greenpeace, the National Toxics Campaign, the National Wildlife Federation, and the Natural Resources Defense Fund joined with Third World development advocates, consumer and farmer organizations, and the Fair Trade Campaign to form a Working Group on Trade and Environmentally Sustainable Development. It worked to focus congressional attention on environmental and other deleterious dimensions of the free trade juggernaut.

The anti-GATT forces stressed the undemocratic character of the whole GATT procedure. The U.S. positions were formulated in secret; the GATT negotiations, too, were conducted in secret. The agencies responsible for enforcing GATT rules are re-moved from democratic accountability. They also criticized the special "fast-track" procedure under which the GATT agreement was to be presented to Congress, which required a vote within 90 days and forbade all amendments. While treaties require a two-thirds majority vote in Congress, GATT was defined as a mere "agreement" needing only a simple majority vote. Yet it would nullify any existing legislation that might conflict with it. In the fall of 1990, more than a third of U.S. senators co-sponsored legis-lation to remove the GATT agreement from the fast-track proce-dures to allow debate and amendment.

International anti-GATT efforts came to a head at a huge demonstration at what were supposed to be the final GATT ne-gotiations in Brussels in December 1990. Says Ritchie,

> So far as I know it was the first really global demonstration, with farmers, environmentalists, and consumer repre-sentatives from every continent organized to affect a global process. There were more than 100 farmers from North America, 200 from Japan, and delegations from Korea, Af-rica, and Latin America. There were a thousand busses from all over Europe, Norway to Greece—more than 30,000 peo-ple. The result was that Thursday night, when the United States made its big push for a free trade agreement, South Korea, Japan, and Europe all said no and they decided to adjourn.

Amazingly, an international people's movement had forced the world's leading governments and their global corporate back-ers into deadlock.[33]

After three years of languishing negotiations (during which U.S. trade activists were engaged in a vigorous fight over NAFTA), negotiators signed an agreement at the end of 1993 re-placing GATT with a World Trade Organization (WTO) and greatly expanding its powers and scope. Throughout 1994, mobi-lizations to fight it were under way in many parts of the world.

NAFTA. Prior to 1990, links among citizen groups in Can-ada, Mexico, and the United States were few. But as North

American economic integration grew, and as hints of a continental trade agreement appeared, hundreds of people in dozens of different geographical and social locations began to take previously unprecedented initiatives. For example:

- groups at universities near the international borders invited people from different countries to conferences on economic integration.

- a U.S. labor activist moved to Mexico and began organizing contacts and visits between U.S. and Mexican workers in the same industries and occupations.

- U.S. local unionists organized support and speaking tours for fired and blacklisted Mexican unionists.

- several small centers were started to promote dialogue and communication between citizens in the United States, Mexico, and Canada.

- Religious and trade union groups in the United States and Mexico organized a "Coalition for Justice in the Maquiladoras" to mobilize pressure on both sides of the border to force corporations to improve labor, environmental, and social conditions in the maquiladora zones.

- Women in the United States and Mexico organized an on-going series of discussions about the conditions of women in the two countries, paying special attention to the impact of economic integration on women, and published the results in a series of newsletters.

- Thirty Canadians met with seventy Mexicans in Mexico City to discuss trade agreements and related issues. The delegations included trade unionists, environmentalists, and representatives of women's, farm, indigenous peoples, human rights, and other movements. Billed as an "encounter," the meeting agreed to establish a commission to mobilize opposition to a free trade agreement in both countries, develop alternative approaches to economic cooperation, and organize a follow-up meeting with representatives from popular organizations in the United States, as well.

- The very week before negotiations for a trade agreement were announced, 53 official national and/or regional representatives of trade unions, agricultural worker organizations, environmental groups, immigrant rights organizations, Latino communities, grassroots development groups, academic specialists, and policy analysts from Mexico and the United States met in Austin, Texas for a "Binational Exchange" on economic integration.

When Presidents Bush and Salinas announced that they would negotiate a free trade agreement and Canada asked to participate as well, these trinational citizen initiatives intensified. In the United States, a coalition of labor, farm, development, environmental, religious, and consumer groups organized a one-day Congressional Forum in Washington where sessions on labor, environment, and agriculture featured speakers from the United States, Mexico, and Canada. Farm groups in the three countries began sending delegations of farmers to each others' meetings and developing a common critique of the impact of NAFTA on family farmers and farm policy in each country. The anti-NAFTA coalitions in each country began regularly inviting representatives from the other two countries to their major conferences, demonstrations, and lobbying events and consulting with each other about their policy approaches and strategy so as not to undermine each others' efforts.

Canada already had a strong coalition, the Action Canada Network (ACN), which had developed in 1987 to fight the earlier U.S.-Canada free trade agreement. It included women's groups, churches, farmers, unions, small business groups, indigenous peoples, youth, environmentalists, and others. Its initial strategy, according to Canadian activist Ken Trainer, was "to get every organization in the country that had a public policy agenda to look at the implications of the trade agreement for their objectives.

That was very successful in bringing them all to a common opposition to the agreement." According to Elaine Bernard, a Canadian labor activist who now heads the Harvard University Trade Union Program, "For two years the trade agreement was the overwhelming issue in the entire country—I've never seen anything like it except the Vietnam war debate in the United States." The result, according to Bernard, was a deep reconsideration of the values of Canadian society. "It led Canadians to pose the question: What sort of society do we want to be? And overwhelmingly the answer has been, we don't want to be a society based purely on the pursuit of profit; we want to be one in which values of caring and community are recognized and expressed in our political life—a society that puts people first."[34] As Canada joined the United States and Mexico in negotiations for a continental agreement, the ACN quickly joined the battle against NAFTA.

In Mexico's repressive political atmosphere, opposition to NAFTA was difficult. A courageous group of environmental, independent trade union, human rights, women's, farm, and other oragnizations nonetheless formed the Mexican Action Network on Free Trade (R-MALC), which challenged the government's claims that NAFTA would benefit Mexico and provided a Mexican voice in transnational citizen discussions.

In the United States, the Fair Trade Campaign initiated by small farm advocates to fight GATT quickly moved into the anti-NAFTA struggle. Inside the beltway, an ad hoc coalition of national organizations came within a few votes of defeating fast track authority for NAFTA. The drive against the fast track grew into a multi-faceted campaign. At the grassroots, local groups such as the Kansas City Maquiladora Task Force, the Minnesota Fair Trade Coalition, the Tennessee Industrial Renewal Network, and the Los Angeles Coalition for Fair Trade and Economic Justice organized local actions to influence the NAFTA negotiations. Nationally, a coalition including the AFL-CIO, several unions, American Agricultural Movement, National Family Farm Coalition, Friends of the Earth, Methodist Church, Public Citizen, National Consumers League, and many other organizations pushed to defeat NAFTA or replace it with a different kind of continental agreement.

Many activities stressed transnational cooperation. Caravans of big trucks organized by the Teamsters union which toured California making the case against NAFTA always included Mexican workers, who talked about how they, too, were losers under trade rules that lacked labor and environmental protections. One southern state was toured by workers from Mexican maquiladora plants that had been transferred from that state.[35] An informal survey of U.S. anti-NAFTA organizers found that more than half had participated in sending and hosting transnational delegations and other forms of international solidarity activity.[36]

Several transnational organizations linked particular constituencies, such as Mujer a Mujer/Woman to Woman and the North American Worker-to-Worker Network. Computer communications became a crucial vehicle for linking efforts in the three countries. As one international labor networker wrote, "We communicate regularly with unionists in the three countries, as well as with organizations working against the free trade agreement. Online networking has been essential to our trinational organizing of conferences, exchanges, and tours. We have regularly exchanged information about events and contacts. The updates on NAFTA have been key to our networking with the North American Worker to Worker Network."[37]

In five meetings over the course of two years, representatives from environmental, labor, religious, consumer, and farm groups in Mexico, the United States, and Canada negotiated an unprecedented alternative plan for the North American economy: *A Just and Sustainable Trade and Development Initiative for North America*. It defines an agenda for the future of the North American economy based on "respect for basic human rights, the promotion of democracy, citizen participation in decision-making, environmental sustainability, and the reduction of economic inequalities among and within our countries."[38]

Continental solidarity activities continue despite the passage of NAFTA. The anti-NAFTA coalition in one North Central state mobilized a caravan of material aid to Mexican union organizers to show their continuing commitment. U.S. and Canadian activists supported human rights protections for the indigenous uprising in Chiapas, sending delegations, holding rallies and public education events in U.S. and Canadian cities, and maintaining sustained demonstrations at Mexican consulates in several California cities. Several unions have created "strategic alliances" across North American borders. Citizens' groups across North America have protested attacks by Mexican police on workers at Sony, GE, and elsewhere. Trade activists have begun grassroots monitoring of the effects of NAFTA. Tri-national meetings have continued—now joined by representatives of popular organizations in countries like Chile that are considered candidates for joining NAFTA.

The Building Blocks of a Movement

From the IMF riots to the Zapatista uprising in Chiapas, from voter rejection of structural adjustment and shock therapy to general strikes against the dismantling of labor protections, the effects of globalization have met worldwide protest. These expressions of resistance have begun to link up by means ranging from grassroots person-to-person cross-border visitations to transnational computer networks to the NGO counter-meetings at the annual gatherings of the World Bank and IMF. And they have begun to develop counter-programs for the governance of the international economy, such as the program of the Fifty Years Is Enough Campaign and *A Just and Sustainable Trade and Development Initiative for North America*. While there is no way to count, surely tens of millions of people have participated in such actions. These initiatives form potential building blocks for a worldwide movement to resist downward leveling—a movement for globalization-from-below.

Chapter Six

The Lilliput Strategy

How can those who wish to oppose downward leveling do so effectively? Many routes seem closed. Local and national governments, political parties, trade unions, grassroots organizations, farm, environmental, and other advocacy groups all have been outflanked by global corporations and markets. International economic institutions like the World Bank, IMF, and GATT provide few mechanisms by which they can be held accountable. There is no global government to legislate on behalf of the world's people.

One starting point for a solution lies in expanding transnational citizen action. Just as genuine democracy at a local and national level depends upon people organizing themselves and acting independently of government—in what is often now called "civil society"—so transnational citizen action is the key to meeting the problems of globalization. Indeed, citizen action is even more crucial in the global realm because the institutions of governance there are so limited and so undemocratic. Those threatened by globalization are almost entirely excluded from influence in the emerging global realm. Transnational citizen action is the means by which they can start affecting the global players and eventually change the rules of the game.

Such action, as we saw in the previous chapter, is already under way. But in most instances it remains fragmented and ineffective. To transform common problems and common interests into common goals and action, and to construct a force that can counter downward leveling, we propose what we call the "Lilliput Strategy."

In Jonathan Swift's satiric fable *Gulliver's Travels*, the tiny Lilliputians, only a few inches tall, captured the marauding Gulliver, many times their height, by tying him down with hundreds of threads while he slept. Gulliver could have crushed any Lilliputian under the heel of his boot—but the dense network of threads tied around him held him immobile and powerless. Similarly, facing powerful global forces and institutions, people can utilize the relatively modest sources of power available to them and combine them with often quite different sources of power available to other participants in other movements and locations. As the tiny Lilliputians captured Gulliver by tying him with many small pieces of thread, the Lilliput Strategy weaves many particular actions designed to prevent downward leveling into a system of rules and practices which together force upward leveling.

In some ways, the Lilliput Strategy parallels the new strategies pursued by global corporations. Just as the corporate strategy creates worldwide production networks linking separate companies, the Lilliput Strategy envisions strong local grassroots organizations that embed themselves in a network of mutual aid and strategic alliances with similar movements around the globe. And just as the corporate strategy seeks to create governance structures at local, regional, national, and transnational levels to support its interests, so the Lilliput Strategy seeks to establish rules protecting the interests of those whom globalization threatens.

Guidelines for Lilliputian Linking

The Lilliput Strategy requires a high level of cooperation among people who are diverse and distant and who have conflicting as well as common interests. These include geographical and historical conflicts between countries and regions; divergence among constituencies and concerns; and gaps between different social spheres, such as the split between economic and political institutions. Overcoming such divisions will require synergistic win-win approaches, mutually beneficial compromises, and agreements to disagree but still cooperate. It is not just a task for a few leaders, but for thousands and ultimately millions of people operating on their own initiative. For at the core of the Lilliput Strategy lies the work of overcoming divisions by constructing links.

• Linking Self-Interest with Common Interests

Most individuals are largely powerless in the face of economic forces beyond their control. But because millions of other people are affected in the same way, they have a chance to influence their conditions through collective action. To do so, people must grasp that the common interest is also their own personal interest. This happens whenever individuals join a movement, a union, a party, or any organization pursuing a common goal. It happens when people push for a social objective—say universal health care or human rights—which benefits them by benefiting all those similarly situated. It underlies the development of an environmental movement which seeks to preserve the environment on which all depend.

While free market ideology may debunk the idea of common or social interests, in effect maintaining—to paraphrase Margaret Thatcher—that only the interests of individuals are real, the linking of self-interest and common interests is the starting point for effective resistance to downward leveling. For example, when people in one country support the right of workers to organize and strike in other countries, they are helping others, but they are also helping themselves by ensuring that they will not have to compete with those forced to work in degraded conditions.

- ## Linking the Global to the Local

To link self-interest with common global interests, the first step is to clarify the connections between the immediate conditions people face and the global processes that are affecting them. For example, as part of the campaign against ratification of GATT, the Sierra Club published the study GATT Double Jeopardy: State Environmental Laws at Risk[1] which provides state-by-state information on how GATT could undermine recycling, packaging, fuel efficiency, and food safety laws. Similarly, in the long and bitter struggle of workers at the Caterpillar tractor company, the union made clear the international dimension; as one UAW official explained, "Cat would like to force workers in different countries to compete with one another to see who will work for the lowest wage."[2] In both these instances, the link between local problems and the forces promoting downward leveling were made clear.

The second step is to link local struggles with global support. A classic example is the international network of indigenous peoples, environmental activists, and trade unionists who supported the struggles of Chico Mendes and the indigenous Amazonian rubber tappers, ultimately forcing the World Bank to shift its development policies in the Amazon rainforest. In the case of the Caterpillar workers, the International Metalworkers Federation convened a world conference of Caterpillar workers in Peoria, Illinois. UAW Secretary-Treasurer Bill Casstevens declared, "In the struggle to win a fair contract at Caterpillar, we need to reach across national borders."[3] In sum, resist downward harmonization where you are and help others resist it where they are.

The third step is to link local problems to global solutions. For example, the International Labor Organization (ILO), a UN affiliate, has developed an International Labor Code—but the United States has refused to ratify most of the conventions that make up the Code. The Code would forbid many of the worst U.S. labor abuses, such as sweatshop child labor and the firing of union activists. In one recent case before the ILO, the AFL-CIO charged the United States with violating international labor standards by denying full bargaining rights to public employees. In 1993 the ILO upheld the charge that U.S. laws do not meet the "requirements of the principle of voluntary collective bargaining"—indicating how an international labor rights system with teeth could provide a "court of appeals" for abuses here at home.

• Linking North and South

Downward leveling hurts people in countries at every level of development, generating a common interest among the majority in both rich and poor countries. Yet globalization itself creates barriers to cooperation between First and Third World countries and movements. First World attempts to limit job loss can easily take an anti-Third World form, for example by excluding Third World products from First World markets; low-wage workers in Third World countries can appear to be "stealing" First World jobs.

Latin American political scientist Jorge Castañeda has proposed a "Grand Bargain" between First and Third World countries which illustrates what it means to seek win-win solutions to this division. Castañeda notes that "global interdependence gives the poorer nations of the South leverage they never had before" and "competition among the northern powers is also more intense," making a "Grand Bargain between North and South" possible.[4]

Castañeda observes that the 1992 Rio Earth Summit did not establish such a bargain, but the positions of the parties pointed toward one. "Both sides of the globe had an agenda. The North sought southern cooperation on protection of forests and access to biological resources, and on the broader issue of sustainable development...The developing nations' agenda was equally concrete: funding from the North for sustainable development in general, for next century's Agenda 21 cleanup program, through implementation of the principle that the polluter pays, and for sharing proceeds from the South's biodiversity more equitably."

Castañeda suggests that a similar basis for bargaining exists for economics.

> The agreement must entail a return to nonreciprocal policies and differentiated market access, in compensation for the implementing of environmental and social policies in the Third World that deter jobs from fleeing en masse from the high-wage countries to the low-wage ones, while at the same time ensuring more job creation and investment in the Third World countries than would occur otherwise...In exchange for not leaving their markets totally unprotected...the nations of Latin America should establish social and environmental controls in their export sectors conforming to norms followed in the industrialized nations. Exports would grow at a reasonable pace, domestic markets would remain protected in some areas, and not so many jobs would be displaced from North to South. The added benefit of such a compromise is that it might make sustainable development possible.[5]

The starting point for a "Grand Bargain" like that proposed by Castañeda is a dialogue among First and Third World popular movements and organizations. Such a process of dialogue underlay the negotiation of *A Just and Sustainable Trade and Development Initiative for North America*. Those negotiations identified and found resolutions for crucial areas of conflict that are likely to arise in any effort to develop a common agenda for First and Third World peoples. For example, the minimum labor, environmental, and social standards that promote upward leveling are costly for poorer countries. Poor countries will find them difficult to accept unless they are compensated by the rich. In the *Initiative* negotiations, the Mexicans agreed to accept labor rights and standards only on the condition that they be accompanied by compensatory funding and debt reduction.[6]

Such a Grand Bargain requires that people in industrial countries actively support imports from poor countries which maintain appropriate standards. This approach was embodied in an agreement among textile and garment workers unions from all over the Americas who met under the auspices of the International Textile, Garment and Leather Workers' Federation. They developed a joint position paper embodying an alternative to the running battle over the admission of Third World exports to the United States. It proposed that the unions of the hemisphere agree that such imports should be allowed if—and only if—basic human and labor rights such as the right to organize and bargain collectively are protected.[7]

Such a dialogue among popular movements needs to be followed by a similar dialogue among governments. Governance of the global economy cannot be the private province of the world's wealthiest; it must have a structured position for the overwhelming majority of the world who are poor, represented by their governments, popular movements, and other nongovernmental organizations. The Third World Network has called for "a new North-South economic dialogue."[8] Such a process, leading to one or a series of global summits, could create new rules for the world economy. Since the Rio "Earth Summit" dealt extensively with "environment" but precious little with "development," such a dialogue would be a logical follow-up. The "Social Summit" scheduled for 1995 in Copenhagen provides a possible occasion to begin the process.

• Linking Constituencies Across Borders

Many social groups cut across national boundaries, providing important forms of transnational linkage. The women's movement provides valuable examples. An internationally coordinated effort forced the 1993 international human rights conference to incorporate the rights of women as an integral aspect of internationally recognized human rights. International efforts have challenged sex tourism. Mujer a Mujer has linked women in the United States and Mexico to develop common approaches to the exploitation of women on both sides of the border.

The networking organization PP21 stimulates this kind of linking throughout the Asian-Pacific region. For example, groups from Nepal, India, and Bangladesh who met in 1993 to discuss common concerns related to the Ganges River under the auspices of PP21 formed a "trans-border people's alliance" to address economic and ecological problems arising from deforestation.[9]

- ## Linking Particular Identities with Wider Commonalities

Each person is a member of specific groups—geographical, ethnic, racial, gender, national, religious, and the like. At the same time each is affected, both as an individual and as a group member, by wider social forces. For example, downward leveling has an impact on people of color in the United States in the same general way that it does on the population as a whole. But it also has a special impact, since people of color are largely concentrated in the industries and occupations that are most threatened by globalization. Similarly, the "export processing zones" in the Third World employ women disproportionately and under particularly exploitative conditions. The exploitation of these women is a specific concern to women around the world. Resistance to the repression of specific ethnic, national, and religious groups is a struggle for their own freedom, but also part of the broader struggle for human rights. When such linkages are highlighted, the struggles of groups with particular identities can become part of, rather than barriers to, broader cooperation.

- ## Linking Issues and Constituencies

The Lilliput Strategy depends on cooperation among a wide range of movements and constituencies. While there is no automatic confluence of these forces and there is always a possibility for conflict, several dynamics are encouraging such convergence.

Many issues like the environment, consumer protection, or the global economy have impacts far beyond the groups directly involved with them. Therefore common interests often reach far beyond those who currently consider themselves members of a group. You don't have to be an environmentalist to get skin cancer from the destruction of the ozone layer; nor do you have to be a labor rights activist to lose your job to workers who are denied them.

Many constituencies overlap. For example, as women have become a growing proportion of the workforce, a majority of women are also workers, a large proportion of workers are women, and a growing proportion of trade union members are women. While men may hold a disproportionate share of top union jobs, the idea that women are one constituency and workers a different one no longer corresponds to reality.

Individuals who are active members of one movement are also often active supporters of others. The leaders of local anti-NAFTA and other community-labor coalitions in the United States, for example, are often people who have been active in a range of other movements and personally identify with a wide variety of issues, whatever their current organizational affiliation.[10]

There are also specific convergences of philosophy and approach among different movements. Ten years ago, environmental protection and economic development were widely regarded as opposed and incompatible objectives, and the environment and development movements were often seen as antagonists. Over the past decade, the two objectives have increasingly come to be seen as interdependent. Development advocates have come to realize that environmental degradation is a principal barrier to development, while environmentalists have come to realize that poverty is a principal cause of environmental destruction. The widespread acceptance of the concept of "sustainable development," however vague and ambiguous it may be, reflects this convergence. Similar convergences have occurred between feminist and environmental, civil rights and environmental, and human rights and labor rights movements, among others. Such convergences do not eliminate all conflict, but they do provide a basis for cooperation.

- ## Linking the Threatened with the Marginalized

A feature of regulated capitalism in many parts of the world was a sharp division between favored "mainstream" groups who were incorporated into systems providing stable employment and social benefits and those more marginalized groups living in poverty and insecurity with few social protections. This economic division often tracked divisions of race, ethnicity, gender, and nationality. Mainstream and marginal groups were often set against each other politically—in the United States, for example, the mainstream working class was often pitted against what was described as the poor or underclass.

The New World Economy is undermining this division. The protections of the mainstream are eroding—for example, corporate "downsizing" has imposed on professionals and managers an economic insecurity once reserved for blue collar workers. These growing commonalities expand the opportunity for efforts to link the mainstream with the margins.

Successful models come from South Africa and Brazil. In South Africa, it was the combination of the black labor movement, the community-based revolt in the black townships, and the political leadership of the African National Congress, that ultimately brought about the downfall of apartheid. In Brazil, it was the alliance—forged largely in the Workers Party (PT)—of the industrial union movement with the urban and rural poor that set the pace for democratization.

- ## Linking Different Power Sources

Much of the effectiveness of transnational campaigns comes from their ability to link different kinds of power. The campaign to affect World Bank policy in the Amazon, for example, combined the on-the-ground efforts of the rubber tappers and other indigenous people fighting to preserve their environment and livelihood; the large national membership base of environmental organizations in the United States; U.S. legislators who controlled the replenishment process for World Bank funding; the lobbying of their own government by environmental advocacy groups in Brazil; the mobilization of expertise by environmental think tanks and anthropologists, biologists, physicians and other experts; and the influence of dissident personnel within the World Bank itself.[11] The Free South Africa campaign similarly combined community organization in the townships; labor organizing; mass civil disobedience; armed struggle; international grassroots campaigns to force universities, governments, and other institutions to withdraw investments from South Africa; sports and entertainment boycotts; and military and economic sanctions. The "corporate campaign" technique, which has been widely used as an adjunct to strikes and campaigns for corporate responsibility, characteristically combines publicity, job actions, demonstrations, alliance-building, stockholder protests, and pressure on banks and corporations to sever their ties with the target corporation.[12]

- **Linking Struggles Against Targeted Institutions**

    Global institutions often wreak havoc on people in different parts of the world who are not even aware of each other. Over the past decade, many campaigns have begun to link the efforts of such people. For example, the various campaigns against World Bank and IMF policies that came together in 1994 in the "Fifty Years is Enough" campaign connect the financing of environmental destruction, the mass misery caused by structural adjustment programs, and the undermining of democratic self-government that flow from IMF and World Bank programs all over the world. Similarly, for much of the 1980s a boycott against Shell Oil Company linked its heavy investment in South Africa and its union-busting role in the United States. In 1993, Transnationals Information Exchange, a labor networking organization, brought together an international conference on "Car and Society," with workers in both public transportation and the motor industry as well as transportation and environmental experts, to address the global policies of the auto industry.

- ## Linking Resistance with Institutional Change
Most struggles start with the specific problems of particular people in particular places, but are also often instances of more general problems. Linking specific struggles to more basic institutional changes is a crucial aspect of the process of change. For example, the struggles against toxic dumping in poor communities and communities of color in the United States aim to prevent sickness of those directly affected, but they are also part of the movements for environmental protection and social justice. Similarly, the strikes and organizing campaigns of workers in the Philippines, China, Guatemala, Korea, and other repressive countries are efforts to address their immediate problems, but also assertions of basic human rights. The Nestlé boycott sought to save the lives of Third World babies by reducing inappropriate use of substitutes for mothers' milk, but it also put the question of corporate responsibility on the global agenda. Specific fights and campaigns can be conducted in ways that build support for more basic institutional changes.

Linking specific acts of resistance to an alternative program is a way to demonstrate that struggles do not just represent special interests, but rather common human interests.

- ## Linking Economic Issues and Democratization
The centerpiece of the Corporate Agenda has been the elimination of all forms of popular democratic control of the economy. It has done this by dismantling pro-people, pro-environment regulation; creating institutions of economic regulation outside the reach of democratic control; and marginalizing popular representatives in the political process. To make economic change it will be necessary to challenge these political realities—to make a virtual democratic revolution. Conversely, the movement to expand democracy will mean little to most people unless democracy gives them the opportunity to reshape the economic, social, and environmental conditions of their daily lives. The key to

moving people from political apathy to political participation is to make political participation a vehicle for improving daily life.

The Zapatista movement in Chiapas provides an example of this approach. The Zapatistas made very specific demands regarding land distribution, economic development, social services, and cultural rights for the indigenous peoples of Chiapas. But they maintained that even if the Mexican government made concessions, there was no way that it could be held accountable to implementing them as long as it was fundamentally undemocratic. For that reason the Zapatistas made democratic reform of the Mexican political system a basic objective—one they saw as necessary to achieving their economic and social objectives.

* * * * *

No single tactic, campaign, law, or institution is likely to successfully counter downward leveling. The Lilliput Strategy assumes that multiple threads of grassroots action, linking up around the world, are needed to control global pillage. The Lilliput Strategy envisions the construction of a transnational social movement composed of those who resist downward leveling, participate in efforts for upward leveling, and link up with others pursuing the same goals.

Chapter
Seven

Global Rules

NAFTA, GATT, and similar agreements are often described as "rulebooks" for the international economy. Unfortunately, the "rules" they lay down are almost entirely rules to prevent citizens and governments from doing things corporations do not like. In this chapter, we will examine one crucial aspect of the Lilliput Strategy: the effort to inscribe in the global economy rules that protect ordinary people and the environment from corporations and corporate-dominated governments by establishing minimum rights and standards.

Minimum rights and standards are a long-established method of limiting the destructive effects of competition. People apply this approach all the time at the national level. For example, when New York State began pressuring General Electric to stop pouring PCBs into the Hudson River, workers and local communities were terrified that the company would simply move its production elsewhere, devastating the local economy. Their solution was to lobby for federal regulations that would ban PCB pollution for the entire country.

The same approach has long been applied to labor conditions. In the 1920s, for example, when individual states tried to regulate labor standards, companies would threaten to move to other states. When the Great Depression drove the working week to seventy or more hours for some, the Federal government provided *national* minimums through the National Recovery Act and the Fair Labor Standards Act.[1] After World War II, many European nations went even further, setting wage patterns for entire countries by law.

In short, minimum rights and standards were a central feature of nation-based economies and their Keynesian policies for sustaining buying power. Such measures won wide support not only from those who directly benefited, but from the public and often even much of business. They could see that a "race to the bottom" can be so devastating that almost everyone loses in the end.[2] Is it possible to expand such standards beyond the boundaries of individual nations?

There is no world government with the power to pass laws decreeing minimum standards. That makes the task harder, but not impossible. After all, national governments did not always have this power. In the United States, the Supreme Court once forbade even state governments from regulating such matters as minimum wages and hours of labor.[3] Only through long struggles with complex strategies combining legal, legislative, and direct action tactics were governmental institutions enforcing such standards created. Indeed, it is precisely where governments and other institutions fail to meet people's needs that social movements develop non-institutionalized means to meet those needs. As once at the national level, so today transnationally, activists have developed creative ways to promote such standards.

An important, though so far limited, example is the way the environmental movement has pressured governments and international institutions to begin responding to global environmental threats. A variety of international agreements, such as the Antarctica Treaty and conventions for protecting endangered species, have begun to define a global environmental policy. Public pressure on governments also forced them to accede to the Montreal Protocol, which not only set global standards for the phasing out of ozone-destroying industrial chemicals, but also, perhaps for the first time, established trade sanctions as a means for enforcing an environmental agreement.[4]

Corporate Codes of Conduct

One way to establish minimum standards is to set rules for global companies through corporate codes of conduct. Such codes first received wide attention in the international campaign to reform infant formula marketing. When the marketing of infant formula in poor countries led to a decline in breast feeding and consequent malnutrition, a coalition of development, health, and religious groups organized an international boycott of all the products of the leading marketer, the Nestlé Corporation. After several years of international citizen mobilization featuring posters and advertisements vividly portraying the effects of formula-induced malnutrition, Nestlé entered negotiations and formally agreed to a code of conduct restricting infant formula marketing. International citizen groups have continued to monitor the agreement and to mobilize against violations. The infant formula campaign inspired an effort to establish a United Nations Code of Conduct for Transnational Corporations.

Corporate codes of conduct were similarly applied to companies doing business in apartheid South Africa. In 1977, Rev. Leon Sullivan devised a code of conduct for U.S. corporations operating in South Africa. Initially the "Sullivan Principles" called for desegregation in the workplace, fair employment practices, equal pay for equal work, training programs, supervisory jobs for nonwhites, and improved school and health facilities. Many anti-apartheid activists regarded them as a mere figleaf for U.S. corporations that wanted to deflect criticism of their South Africa investments. In response, the Sullivan Principles were toughened to include recognition of unions and support for the movement of Black workers. A law passed over President Reagan's veto in

1986 required American companies with more than twenty-five employees to follow a code of conduct based on the Sullivan Principles.[5]

• The Maquiladora Code of Conduct

A group of U.S. and Mexican organizations has been using the "code of conduct" idea to challenge the policies of foreign corporations setting up plants in Mexico. Long before NAFTA, U.S. and other foreign companies had established 1,800 "maquiladora" factories employing nearly half-a-million Mexican workers, 80 percent of them women, on the U.S. border. Wages in the maquiladoras, according to *Business Week*, were half those in the rest of Mexico—and one-tenth those in the United States. The *Wall Street Journal* reported "abysmal living conditions and environmental degradation."

The Coalition for Justice in the Maquiladoras was formed to raise the standards for maquiladora workers and their communities. Their mission statement declared,

> We are a binational coalition of religious, environmental, labor, Latino and women's organizations that seek to pressure U.S. transnational corporations to adopt socially responsible practices within the maquiladora industry, that will ensure a safe environment on both sides of the border, safe work conditions inside the maquila plants and a fair standard of living for the industry's workers.

The Coalition developed a "Maquiladora Standards of Conduct" to provide "a code through which we demand that corporations alleviate critical problems created by the industry." Its 22 provisions address a wide range of the abuses found in the maquiladoras.

The code spells out provisions for environmental protection, such as disclosure of all toxic chemical discharges, use of state-of-the-art environmental control technologies, and return of all hazardous materials to country of origin. It requires that workers be notified of hazardous materials and that worker-management health and safety commissions be established. It bans employment discrimination based on sex, age, race, religious creed, or political beliefs; requires equal pay for equal work; protects workers' right to organize; and demands disciplinary measures against sexual harassment. It discourages barrack-style living arrangements, demands regular inspection of existing barracks by an internationally recognized human rights organization, and requires corporate contributions to trust funds for infrastructure improvements in maquiladora communities. The code incorporates many labor and environmental standards already required by Mexican law but poorly enforced in the maquiladoras.

The Coalition has engaged in a series of campaigns against such companies as the Stepan Chemical Company, Ford, and Becton, Dickinson. Its exposé of toxic flows from GM plants into Mexican water supplies was largely responsible for GM's 1991 decision to spend $17 million to build water treatment plants at its thirty-five maquiladora plants.

The coalition also mobilizes support for workers victimized by companies in the maquiladoras. In April 1994, for example, when workers demonstrating for fair union elections and an end to compulsory Saturday and Sunday work at a Sony plant in Nuevo Laredo were beaten by Mexican police, members of the Coalition immediately mobilized a letter-and-fax campaign to pressure Sony officials in Mexico, the United States, and Japan.

- ## Sourcing Guidelines

A number of corporations have begun to develop codes of conduct for their own and their subcontractors' workplaces. The best known are the sourcing guidelines of Levi Strauss & Co., the world's largest clothing manufacturer.

Peter Jacobi, President of Levi Straus International, recalls, "At a factory in Mexico, workers were exposed to bare wiring with no insulation whatsoever. Female workers in Costa Rica were fired if they became pregnant. When I questioned the contractors about such practices, the response was always, if the competitors fired pregnant women, the employer was forced to fire them in order to stay in business. Such a discrepancy of standards is incompatible with the values of Levi Strauss & Co."[6]

Under its Global Sourcing Guidelines, Levi Strauss & Co. now requires that its contractors abide by the following criteria:

- Child labor is prohibited

- Prison labor is prohibited

- The work environment must be safe and healthy

- Water effluence must be limited to certain prescribed levels

- Employees cannot work more than sixty hours a week and must be allowed one day off in seven

- Business partners must comply with legal business requirements

(The code does not require a living wage or the right to union representation.) Audits of its 700 contractors concluded that 5 percent should be dropped and 25 percent needed to make improvements; Levi Strauss has provided help in meeting the code.

Levi Strauss has also adopted Country Selection Guidelines for factors that are beyond the ability of individual contractors to control, such as impact on brand image, adoption of health and safety requirements, commitment to human rights and legal requirements, and the level of political and social stability. The company has already left Myanmar (formerly Burma) and is phasing out sourcing in China (thus forgoing the world's largest market) due to pervasive human rights abuses.

Several other large corporations have adopted sourcing guidelines, but their products may continue to be produced under horrific conditions nonetheless. Nike, for example, has adopted sourcing guidelines, yet it pays its women workers in Indonesia only $1.30 per day; requires them to work as much as 12 hours per day; and houses them in barracks which they can leave only on Sunday, with a permission letter from management.[7] For sourcing guidelines to be effective, they require effective auditing and enforcement.

Sourcing guidelines have also been imposed on employers by unions. For example, the Amalgamated Clothing and Textile Workers Union (ACTWU) is powerfully organized in the United States tailored clothing industry and has until recently blocked all imports. To allow companies to fill out their product lines, however, the ACTWU's latest contract lets them import up to 10 percent of what they produce in the United States. U.S. companies pay $1 per garment to a pension fund, so that U.S. workers share in the benefit. U.S. companies can only contract with suppliers that accept internationally recognized labor rights and pay a living wage. They must inform the union what contractors they purchase from and guarantee the union's right to inspect their factories. Says ACTWU economist Ron Blackwell, "This policy makes the companies model employers in their countries. It also protects workers who want to organize—and the union expects to try to help them organize."[8]

International Worker Rights

It once was a crime to organize a union or call a strike in the United States and most other countries. Trade unionists were regularly fired, blacklisted, beaten, arrested, and sometimes murdered. Establishing the rights to assemble, organize, bargain collectively, strike, and participate in the political process was the focus of a century of struggle. That struggle was fought on the ground, strike by strike, region by region, and industry by industry; it was also fought in courts and legislatures in an effort to establish and enforce these rights as the law of the land. That struggle continues; in the United States, for example, thousands of workers are fired every year for trying to organize unions.[9]

From Korea to Kenya and from Chile to China, workers in much of the world are today struggling to establish these same rights. An international labor rights movement has developed to support them. Like Amnesty International and other well-known human rights organizations, it publicizes abuses and mobilizes support for the victims. Beyond that, it aims to incorporate labor rights requirements in national and international trade, investment, and lending policies.

- ## Labor Rights in History
In a sense, the first great struggle for international labor rights was the worldwide movement for the abolition of slavery. Abolitionism was driven both by moral and human rights concerns and by the fear of the downward pull that slavery would exert on the conditions of free labor. After a protracted struggle it succeeded in freeing millions of slaves and abolishing what was at the time one of the world's most venerable forms of property.

The struggle for the eight-hour day—a basic labor standard—galvanized the international labor movement throughout the 19th century. May Day became an international workers' holiday in commemoration of a general strike for the eight-hour day in Chicago and other American cities a little over a century ago. The demand for the eight-hour day unified workers across craft, ethnic, and even national boundaries.[10]

- ## The International Labor Organization
The victors of World War I, spooked by the Bolshevik revolution in Russia and fearing the spread of labor radicalism, included a list of worker rights in the Treaty of Versailles. These included the right of association, a wage "adequate to maintain a reasonable standard of life," the principle that men and women should receive "equal remuneration for work of equal value," and the eight-hour day for which the labor movement had so long striven.[11]

They also established an institution to implement these rights, the International Labor Organization. The ILO has a tripartite structure in which each member nation receives four votes, two for government, one for employers, and one for workers. After World War II, the ILO was incorporated into the United Nations system. At present 169 nations belong.[12]

Over the course of seventy-five years, the ILO has established 174 "Conventions" defining basic labor rights and standards. The first dealt with hours of work, the most recent with the prevention of major industrial accidents. The Conventions go through a lengthy review process and must be passed by a two-thirds vote. Conventions cover basic human rights (such as freedom of association, abolition of forced labor, and elimination of discrimination in employment), minimum wages, labor administration, industrial relations, employment policy, working conditions, social security, occupational safety and health, and women workers.[13] Where appropriate, the standards are adjusted for countries with different levels of development.

When a country ratifies a Convention it makes a formal commitment to apply its provisions and to accept a measure of international supervision. (The United States has voted for most Conventions, but has ratified only eleven.) While they are only legally binding on countries that ratify them, the Conventions, together with non-binding Recommendations, form an International Labor Code that provides a widely-accepted definition of labor standards.[14] The ILO has no enforcement powers, but its official committees review national labor laws and alleged violations of basic labor rights and report their findings; since 1964, nearly 2,000 changes in national law and practice have been reported in response to ILO supervisory bodies.

• The Labor Rights Movement

In the 1980s, the growing international human rights movement, combined with globalization of the economy, led to the rise of a new international labor rights movement. The labor rights approach tied together two important themes: the democratic concern with human rights and the need of workers for a level international playing field in which wages cannot be kept low through repression.

The tremendous success of Amnesty International and other human rights organizations in bringing human rights issues to international attention offered a strategic model. Just as various UN declarations and agreements defined standards for human rights, so the International Labor Code of the ILO provided standards for labor rights.[15] Publicity could be used both to curb the worst violators and build support for the standards. Public mobilization could build pressure for enforcement—both on the perpetrators and on countries and institutions that could affect them.

A classic example was the international campaign to pressure 3M and the South African government to release Amon Msane, chief steward at the 3M plant near Johannesburg, from prison. With the cooperation of many organizations, thousands of letters were written, company offices were picketed, and 3M officials lobbied. Msane was freed after 50 weeks; he attributed his release to the pressure of this campaign.

Similarly, when Salvadoran union official Humberto Centeno was seized and beaten by the Salvadoran air force, local unions all over the United States were immediately alerted. Within one day, 60 members of Congress were contacted, 1,000 telegrams were sent to the U.S. embassy and the Salvadoran government, and demonstrations were held in five cities. The next day Centeno was released.

Such efforts continue—with increasing support from modern communications technology. On the night of October 3, 1993, for example, Moscow police arrested three leading members of the Russian Party of Labor. They were systematically beaten to try to get them to confess to killing two policemen. The next night the wife of one discovered where they were and contacted a union officer. Within minutes, a message appealing for protest calls was posted via E-mail on a series of international computer conferences. Boris Kagarlitsky, one of those imprisoned, later described what happened.

"We were watching from the cell as the phone calls came in. One of the first was from Japan. The police didn't seem able to believe it. After that, the calls seemed to be coming from everywhere—there were quite a few from the [San Francisco] Bay Area in the United States."

When police told the callers that the prisoners had been released, the prisoners yelled at the top of their lungs that they were still being held. Within a few hours, most of the detainees were released and the frame-up charges were abandoned.[16]

• Labor Rights and Trade

In the early 1980s, labor rights advocates began focusing on trade policy and international trade agreements as vehicles for enforcement. Tying labor rights to trade was not entirely unprecedented: Nearly a century before, for example, the McKinley Tariff of 1890 had prohibited imports manufactured by convict labor.[17] The linkage of labor rights to trade got an inadvertent push in 1982 when the Polish government banned the Solidarity union. The next day U.S. President Ronald Reagan said Polish officials "have made it clear that they never had any intention of restoring one of the most elemental human rights—the right to belong to a free trade union."[18] The United States retaliated by withdrawing Poland's most-favored-nation status.[19]

In 1983, a coalition of labor unions and human rights organizations formed the International Labor Rights Working Group. Their first target was the Generalized System of Preferences (GSP), a program designed to encourage economic development by reducing tariffs for developing countries. Noting that GSP was encouraging countries like Korea and Taiwan to produce goods for the U.S. market under tyrannical conditions, labor rights advocates in 1984 persuaded Congress to declare a country ineligible for GSP if it "has not taken or is not taking steps to afford internationally recognized worker rights." The rights specified, drawn from key ILO conventions, were:

- the right of association

- the right to organize and bargain collectively

- a prohibition on the use of any form of forced or compulsory labor

- a minimum age for the employment of children

- acceptable conditions of work with respect to minimum wages, hours of work, and occupational safety and health.

Labor rights advocates in the United States, now institutionalized as the International Labor Rights Education and Research Fund (ILRERF), won another victory when Congress in the 1988 Trade Act defined the denial of internationally recognized labor rights as an "unfair and unreasonable trade practice" against which unilateral action could be taken under international trade rules. Denial of labor rights was declared, in effect, "social dumping."[20]

Former Secretary of Labor Ray Marshall, President of the ILRERF, indicated the aspirations of labor rights advocates:

> Eventually, the United States could push for all its global trading partners to protect freedom of association, permit collective bargaining and prohibit forced labor. Also, foreign nations could be called on to establish a minimum age for employment and impose acceptable standards for wages, hours and occupational safety and health.[21]

So far, most U.S. government evaluations of labor rights violations have been patently political, marked by the same double-standard hypocrisy that characterizes so much official human rights policy. The first countries cut off by the Reagan Administration were Rumania, Nicaragua, and Paraguay. For obviously political reasons, the Reagan Administration rejected petitions calling for reviews of labor practices of such blatant violators (but U.S. "friends") as El Salvador, Guatemala, Indonesia, Thailand, Turkey, and the Philippines. The ILRERF and 22 other labor and human rights groups sued top government officials for failure to comply with the law, but the presiding judge dismissed the case, refusing to interfere with "the President's discretionary authority in a broad area of foreign relations" or to "resolve broad issues of public policy that are properly only the special concern of Congress."

President Clinton seemed to have a better grasp of the significance of labor rights. "Okay, if we're going to open our borders and trade more and invest more with developing nations, we want to know that their working people will receive some of the benefits," he said. "Otherwise, they won't have increasing incomes and they won't be able to buy our products and services."[22]

But the Clinton Administration in practice has followed the same course as the Reagan and Bush Administrations. For example, unable to ignore evidence of labor rights repression in Indonesia presented in petitions submitted by labor and human rights groups, the U.S. trade representative (USTR) simply announced that its review would be "suspended" for six months, allowing trade privileges to continue despite the arrest a week before of 19 Indonesian trade union leaders for having criticized new government labor regulations.[23] The Clinton administration, reversing its own pledge, provided most favored nation status to China, despite systematic suppression of independent labor organizations, use of prison labor, and other human rights violations.

Labor rights advocates are continuing to use the labor rights provisions of U.S. trade law as a focus for campaigns against labor rights abuses not only in Indonesia and China but also in El Salvador, Honduras, Thailand, Guatemala, Malaysia, and other repressive countries. These campaigns have proved useful for creating links both with trade unionists in these countries and with religious, human rights, international development, and solidarity movements in the United States. Labor rights advocates have also drafted revised legislation eliminating the loopholes that have allowed the government to apply the law so unevenly, and—at the urging of women's groups—adding non-discrimination to the list of basic labor rights.

Experience so far indicates that labor rights provisions in U.S. trade law could have a potent effect—if they were applied consistently. In 1988, for example, the AFL-CIO and human rights groups, working closely with unions in Malaysia, submitted a petition charging that unions were outlawed in the electronics industry there. When the USTR stated it would accept the petition for review, the Malaysian government announced that unions would be permitted in the electronics sector. Within a few days organizing efforts were under way in the electronics plants. But when the USTR ruled Malaysia was "taking steps" to afford worker rights and therefore qualified for GSP, a relieved Malaysian government, under strong electronics industry pressure, restored the union ban.

When the United States announced that it would review Indonesia's GSP trade privileges because of its suppression of labor rights, Indonesia announced a series of steps expanding labor union rights and raising minimum wages. According to *The New York Times*, "No one seriously believes that these steps would have been taken now were it not for the Clinton initiative." But the Administration suspended its review, despite the fact that "Indonesian labor activists still face severe repression, including harsh prison sentences, military intervention in strikes and restrictive rules on union democracy and jurisdiction."[24]

- ## Labor Rights in GATT

For many years, labor rights advocates have argued for incorporating labor rights provisions in international trade agreements. During the Uruguay Round of GATT negotiations, the United States, under pressure from the labor movement, proposed to establish an international labor rights working party in GATT; the European Parliament recently voted to include labor laws in GATT.[25] Such Third World governments as Mexico, India, Singapore, the Philippines, Thailand, Indonesia, Zaire, Cuba, and Egypt have strenuously objected. The representative of Pakistan said it was "more important to have workers employed than to be concerned with whether they are making one dollar or twenty dollars an hour." South Korea's spokesperson was strongly opposed to a "working party to look at worker rights like freedom of association, [which] should be left to each country to decide for itself."[26]

Third World NGOs and citizen organizations, like Third World governments, often question proposals for labor, environmental, and social standards imposed from abroad.[27] They point out that for hundreds of years, the North has obtained the South's natural resources and labor on unequal and unfair terms. There is a natural suspicion when powerful countries like the

United States seek to "impose" worker rights and other conditions. Some maintain that the concept of rights is part of Western cultural tradition and that the attempt to impose them elsewhere is an expression of cultural imperialism. There is resentment of World Bank and IMF "conditionalities" and a sense that labor rights and similar conditions are just more of the same. There is hostility against some of the types of sanctions proposed, which can be used by rich and powerful countries against poor and weak ones but not the other way around. Perhaps most important of all, these policies are portrayed as a form of disguised protectionism designed to exclude Third World products from industrial country markets. Where the Corporate Agenda has provided poor countries no way to develop except cheap exports, barriers to their exports may prevent development altogether.

The debate on labor rights in trade agreements came to a head early in 1994, when the Clinton administration unexpectedly demanded agreement on establishing a labor rights working party in GATT's reincarnation, the WTO. Said U.S. trade negotiator Micky Kantor,

> This administration has made it clear that we believe that making sure that countries don't use forced labor, have child labor laws that are effective and enforced, and make sure that collective bargaining rights and freedom of association are adhered to are something that have a profound effect on trade, but even more important, if enforced and part of the World Trade Organization, will make sure that we raise the standard of living not only of workers in our hemisphere but around the world.[28]

Third World governments quickly scuttled the proposal. Brazil's GATT negotiator said it was "not acceptable" because worker rights are a matter for national governments to decide; the Association of South East Asian Nations adopted a resolution condemning it.[29]

While such positions could be discounted as expression of undemocratic governments seeking to perpetuate the exploitation of their own workers, it is harder to dismiss the critique that comes from some Third World NGOs. A paper by Martin Khor, director of the Third World Network, for example, strongly condemned the inclusion of labor rights in GATT/WTO. Khor acknowledged that "labor standards and workers' rights are critical issues for developing countries"; that "Workers, their unions and other public organizations in the South have a legitimate right to organize against exploitation"; and that "The fight for better wages and working conditions is a legitimate one, and also a formidable one in many Third World countries, especially where democratic freedoms are absent or severely limited, and where there is a powerful alliance between corporate interests, the landed and propertied elite, bureaucracy and politicians."

But, Khor argued, "The attempt by the U.S. and other industrial countries, particularly France, to introduce 'labour standards' and 'workers' rights' as an issue for the World Trade Organization to take up is quite clearly prompted not by feelings of goodwill toward Third World workers, but by protectionist attempts to prevent the transfer of jobs from the North to the South." Countries which violated WTO standards, he maintained, could be accused of social dumping and face tariffs designed to keep their products out of Northern markets; if Southern countries raised their wages, they might well be priced out of Northern markets anyway.

Khor maintained that GATT/WTO was selected for labor rights enforcement because it is controlled by "a few northern countries or entities" and because trade retaliation provides an enforcement mechanism which rich countries can use against the Third World. He proposed that if a link between worker rights and trade is to be discussed, it should be dealt with instead in the ILO, which has broad experience in such matters and is part of the "more internationally democratic United Nations framework." Meanwhile, northern governments should stop making the South a scapegoat for their own unemployment problem and instead address their own problems with technological change and macroeconomic imbalance.[30]

Many labor rights advocates in the North share Martin Khor's scepticism regarding the motivation of the U.S. labor rights initiative. But they point out that the race to the bottom has devastating impact on Third World as well as First World countries. The absence of minimum standards is not just a problem for the North; it poses a crucial threat to development programs in the South as well. Their workforces are also being put into ruinous competition. For that reason, as well as for their own protection, trade unionists in such Third World countries as Malaysia, Pakistan, and Ghana support international labor rights.[31]

Labor rights advocates have suggested a number of approaches, many of them growing out of the U.S.-Mexico-Canada citizens negotiations for an alternative to NAFTA, which may contribute to the development of an approach which addresses the needs of ordinary people in both North and South:[32]

- Distinguish "rights" to which every individual, every worker, and every group should be entitled from "standards" which should be adjusted to the actual capacities of different societies and nations and should rise as those capacities increase.

- Provide compensatory funds so that poor countries don't have to pay the cost of upward leveling.

- Enforce agreements not by punitive trade sanctions against industries or countries, which encourage protectionism and punish the wrong people, but by fines against corporations or reparations from violators to victims.

- Utilize the ILO, with its long experience in setting standards and reviewing compliance, to determine violations.

- Require that dispute resolution mechanisms provide citizen standing to bring petitions and open and fair dispute resolution not subject to rich-country domination.[33] National approaches should be used only to create pressure for adoption of multilateral ones.

- Enforce international labor rights and standards not just in developing countries but in the United States and other industrialized countries.

There is a parallel between international labor rights and the development of concern with environmental protection. The environmental movement was once widely perceived as anti-Third World. Poor countries, it was often alleged, were only concerned with "development" and couldn't afford the luxury of concern with "environment." This view changed as more and more people and governments recognized that environmental enhancement was necessary for development and that poverty was a principal cause of environmental degradation. But the fact remained that environmental protection is costly for poor countries. In the discussions leading up to the Rio Earth Summit, many Southern NGOs and Northern environmental groups came to a common view that environmental protection is essential, but that it must be paid for by the rich countries that can afford it and will receive much of the benefit. A similar North/South/labor/NGO dialogue on international labor rights could form the starting point for a "Grand Bargain" linking the interests of workers in more and less developed countries.[34]

The EU Social Dimension

A possible model for imposing pro-social rules on the New World Economy comes from the European Union (EU)—undoubtedly the world's most advanced experiment in international integration. Wary that jobs might rush to the poorest regions of an integrated Europe, the architects of the EU decided to include a "Social Dimension." Minimum labor standards were spelled out in the 1988 Social Charter and expanded in the "Social Chapter" of the Maastricht Treaty of 1991. (The United Kingdom has been allowed to opt out of the labor standards agreements—which Margaret Thatcher condemned as a "throwback to Marxism.") The Social Dimension also includes "structural funds" which provide resources to compensate poorer member states for the possible cost of meeting EC standards.[35]

While the Social Dimension is still in an early stage of development, limitations are apparent. It provides minimum labor standards, but leaves labor rights to other forums. Its standards are not fully developed and some are quite low, though others are higher than existing standards in poorer countries like Greece or even Britain. (They are particularly strong in the areas of health, safety, and women's rights.) The effectiveness of the enforcement mechanism, based on the European Court of Justice and, below it, the courts of member governments, has not yet been tested. Some of the potentially significant innovations, such as the provision for EU-level company works councils, are just beginning. The decision to let Britain opt out of the labor standards agreement encourages just the downward leveling the standards were designed to forestall.[36] More broadly, the entire EU system suffers from a top-down, "Eurocratic" decision-making process and its focus has shifted from upward leveling via Europe-wide minimum standards to downward leveling via rules requiring national governments to admit all imports that meet EU standards, even if they violate higher national standards.

Nonetheless, the Social Dimension is highly significant in that it recognizes the fundamental problem of downward leveling and creates a possible framework for addressing it. The way it is being implemented inevitably reflects the real balance of forces, in which corporations and their owners are far more powerful than labor and other non-elite groups. But it does indicate one kind of institutional structure that could begin to counter the race to the bottom.

A Global Social Charter

Halting the race to the bottom and encouraging upward leveling require minimum labor, environmental, and social standards worldwide. According to labor rights advocate John Cavanagh, these standards should be made "part of both national and international law and policy, a condition that must be met to get the benefits of GATT, the World Bank, and access to other country's markets."

The cumulative effect would be to establish a world-wide social charter setting a floor under environmental, labor, and social conditions. It would provide both universal rights and rising minimum standards appropriate to countries at different levels of development. It would apply both to countries and to corporations. It would establish institutions for enforcement that would be democratic, open to public participation, and ultimately backed by the power to exclude violators from the benefits of trade, aid, and finance.

The vehicles for reaching this goal include citizen action in civil society and government action in the national and international arenas. Citizen action includes international solidarity support, collective bargaining agreements controlling sourcing, and codes of conduct imposed via corporate campaigns and other forms of public pressure. Government action includes national trade and aid laws and policies; national laws regulating corporate behavior; and bilateral, regional, and global trade and investment agreements.[37]

Chapter Eight

Labor in the New World Economy

The institutions and movements ordinary people used to pursue their interests in the era of nation-based economies have so far been unable to halt globalization's downward leveling. Local and national governments, political parties, trade unions, grassroots organizations, farm, environmental, and other advocacy groups—all have been largely outflanked by global corporations, institutions, and markets. All of them have a crucial role to play in reversing the race to the bottom—but they can only play it if they redefine themselves as part of a global effort to change the rules of the game. In this chapter we look at the history, current approaches, and possible future course of organized labor in the United States as an example of the challenges globalization poses to organizations whose function is to represent non-elite groups.

Labor: International and National

Eliminating labor costs as a factor in competition has been an underlying economic goal of the labor movement since its inception. In its earliest stages, this goal was pursued on a local level—shoemakers, blacksmiths, or carriagemakers in a town would get together to set rates so as not to drive each others' wages down. As transportation improved and markets expanded, workers came together to set common rates and standards through national trade unions. They understood that unless they did so, employers would play them against each other in an endless race to the bottom.

Today, as economic competition has become increasingly global, workers in all countries are faced with the threat that someone, somewhere else will do their jobs for less. In response, labor unions around the world are beginning to do on a global scale what they have long tried to do on a national scale—eliminate labor costs as a factor in competition.

Of course, a global strategy cannot be identical to the national labor strategies of the past. There are greater variations in culture, economic conditions, political jurisdictions, and power structures in the world than within any country. New technologies, changing forms of economic organization, and expanded emphasis on such concerns as environmental protection and gender equality mean that all labor strategy, local and national as well as transnational, will be different from the past.

To pursue transnational cooperation, labor movements will often have to function far more independently of their national governments, work more closely with allies in other social movements, and encourage rather than impede the networking activities of their own rank and file. Nonetheless, at the core of labor's strategy must lie the traditional labor orientation toward leveling conditions upward so that they don't instead level downward.

• A Fraternity of Peoples

There is a long if ambiguous tradition of labor internationalism dating back to the birth of the labor movement. In the 19th century, early unionists like shoemakers, carriagemakers, and hatmakers often followed their work from country to country; intellectuals associated with the labor movement were often cosmopolitans who moved from one country to another with ease.

An expanding capitalism seemed to be creating a world market for commodities and labor which both facilitated international labor solidarity and made it necessary.

For early trade unionists, international labor solidarity was both an ethical ideal and an expression of economic self-interest. The connection between international labor competition and the need for solidarity across national borders was captured over a century ago in a letter that a group of British trade unionists—including a painter, joiner, bookbinder, carpenter, and shoemaker—sent to their French counterparts:

> A fraternity of peoples is highly necessary for the cause of labor, for we find that whenever we attempt to better our social conditions by reducing the hours of toil, or by raising the price of labor, our employers threaten us with bringing over Frenchmen, Germans, Belgians and others to do our work at a reduced rate of wages.

> This has been done not from any desire of our continental brethren to injure us, but through a want of regular and systematic communication between the industrious classes of all countries, which we hope to see speedily effected, as our principle is to bring up the wages of the ill-paid to as near a level as possible with that of those who are better renumerated, and not allow our employers to play us off one against the other, and so drag us down to the lowest possible condition, suitable to their avaricious bargaining.[1]

Many early trade unions in the United States were extensions of those in Europe. The first American labor federation, while by no means revolutionary, readily joined the International Working Men's Association founded in 1864—the "First International"—whose statutes, written by Karl Marx, declared "The emancipation of the workers is not a local, nor a national, but an international problem."[2]

- ## Labor Nationalism
In the late 19th century, industrial capitalism transformed the economies of the United States and Western Europe. Old

craft-based production systems were swept aside by new industrial processes. Workers were concentrated into large factories where they faced harsh discipline, low pay, and poor working conditions. They responded by organizing new trade unions. Many radicals in the labor movement believed that the leveling process of the new industrial system in Europe and North America would lead to the development of an international class-conscious working class and world revolution.

But another force was rising, too. During the 19th and 20th centuries, the nation state became the world's dominant institution and nationalism its most potent creed. In the United States, for example, "Americanism" was increasingly counterpoised to "internationalism." National loyalty became the supreme value, and identification with workers elsewhere was defined as subversive.

Despite nationalist pressures, most labor movements remained strongly anti-militarist and retained sympathy with oppressed workers in other countries. But World War I changed all that. In most countries, labor movements supported their national governments against their national enemies, even though it meant killing "fellow workers." Long-time American Federation of Labor (AFL) president Samuel Gompers observed that "One of the most wholesome lessons that the war taught labor was that we must build our program upon facts and not theories. The ties that bind workingmen to the national government are stronger and more intimate than those international ties that unite workingmen of all countries. There was no international organization that could resist war expediency."[3]

Gompers concluded that the way to protect the labor movement was to forge an alliance with the nation state, exchanging a loyal and disciplined labor force for government-mandated recognition of unions. His approach was extraordinarily successful during the war itself; union membership soared as the government protected the AFL's right to organize while suppressing its militant internationalist rival the Industrial Workers of the World. Once the war was over, however, Gompers' strategy proved a disaster: The AFL was decimated by a management counteroffensive—conducted with help from the government.

Despite such setbacks, the U.S. labor movement increasingly pursued a strategy of cooperation with the national government. The industrial unions that burgeoned in the 1930s avidly promoted nationally regulated capitalism and pursued an alliance with the Democratic Party and those sectors of business that wanted a more regulated economic system.[4] By World War II the labor movement had made considerable progress in winning such national policies as the right to organize, bargain collectively, and strike; minimum wages; improved living and working conditions; public welfare measures; policies to promote full employment; and regulation of the labor market.

A similar integration of labor movements into national economic systems took place in much of the world. The result was that, while wherever there was capitalism there was organized labor, the institutional forms of labor organization differed widely, from the highly centralized bargaining of Scandinavia, to the German co-determination system to the decentralized bargaining of the United States. Despite continuing efforts at internationalism, labor was organized nationally.

• Internationalisms: Left and Right

In the wake of World War I, the Russian Revolution created a new global polarity that would shape the world's labor movements for the next half-century. The anti-communist sectors of the labor movement worked closely with the Allied governments to contain the menace of world revolution. In 1920, communist policy split the world's labor movements and brought those sympathetic to communism under the control of the Soviet-dominated Third International.

The Great Depression, the rise of fascism, and World War II did not put an end to this communist/anti-communist polarity but did remove it from center stage. Both tendencies worked side-by-side, if not without conflict, in European popular fronts and in building the new industrial unions in the United States.

In the closing days of World War II, labor leaders like Sidney Hillman of the newer U.S. labor federation, the Congress of Industrial Organizations (CIO), sought to make a place for labor in post-War reconstruction. Allied with politicians in the Democratic Party like Vice-President Henry Wallace, they articulated a global program rooted in their experience of the New Deal. According to historian Stephen Fraser:

> In the minds of people like Hillman and Wallace, the good health of the New Deal was bound up with the triumph of democracy abroad, while the victory of the global anti-Fascist alliance would count for far less than it might unless the principles of New Deal reform and redistribution were exported throughout Western Europe and the "third world".

Vice-President Wallace projected

> a new world economy based on full employment, a universally recognized decent standard of living, the dismantling of international cartels, free trade, equal access to raw materials, and a global investment fund with which to foster the reindustrialization of Europe and the infrastructural development of the postcolonial world.[5]

This vision of a global New Deal, a kind of "international Keynesian cooperative commonwealth," warmly anticipated anticolonial revolution "as part of the eschatology of antifascism." It proposed "a vast reconstruction of the global hinterland through a network of TVAs [Tennessee Valley Authority] and REAs [Rural Electrification Administration] and RFCs [Reconstruction Finance Corporation], through international trade commissions and international investment agencies, through regional and cross-national public works and development agencies, and of course though an international labor standards commission to protect the rights and guarantee the purchasing power of the world's working classes...The liquidation of the great cartels and monopolies and the installation of universally recognized regulatory standards would pacify the perennially troubled relationship between capitalism and democracy." A new transnational political economy demanded "an apposite response to multinational industry from a multinational working class."[6]

For Hillman and others in the labor movement, such sweeping visions seemed realizable in the glow of the Allied victory. A revitalized international trade union movement would help usher in the new world. In 1945 representatives from trade unions in 56 countries representing 66 million workers met in Paris and founded the World Federation of Trade Unions (WFTU). The WFTU was to be the voice of international labor in post-war reconstruction.

The AFL, in a preview of the coming Cold War, refused to participate in the WFTU's founding because of the presence of communist trade unions. It was the only major trade union organization in the world not to join.

The WFTU was pledged to fighting for full labor and political rights, activist national economic policies, the establishment of cooperatives and mutual aid societies, and an end to racial and gender discrimination in employment, wages, and education. But the unity and vision of the WFTU were soon to run head-on into barriers both national and ideological.

Trade unions, which had long struggled just to survive, were now important national actors unwilling to challenge national governments, which in most countries were supportive of their cause. As Denis MacShane has written, "In 1945 and 1946, unions were reaching the peak of their identification with national interests. French communists were no less patriotic than their American confreres...Of course, the Soviet representatives in the WFTU sought to use their membership to advance Soviet interests, but the British, American, French, and Dutch union leaders equally defended and promoted their countries' positions or interests."[7]

Within the world's labor movements, long-simmering ideological differences dating to the 1920 split between communist and non-communist unions also flared up. The outbreak of the Cold War was the final blow to hopes of genuine post-war labor internationalism. In 1949 the CIO and other Western labor federations left the WFTU on the grounds that it was Soviet-controlled and formed the International Confederation of Free Trade Unions (ICFTU).

- **Labor Internationalism in the Cold War Era**

Curiously enough, the architects of American labor's foreign policy during the Cold War regarded themselves as internationalists—anti-communist internationalists. They cooperated closely with the CIA to break left-led strikes (for example in France in 1949) and overthrow leftist governments (for example in Guatemala in 1954). *Business Week* described the AFL-CIO's global operations, such as its International Affairs Department in Washington and its American Institute for Free Labor Development in Latin America, as "labor's own version of the Central Intelligence Agency—a trade union network existing in all parts of the world."[8]

During the Cold War the AFL-CIO international operation was virtually an arm of U.S. foreign policy, often lending support to dictatorial regimes around the world. Funding came, for the most part, from government sources like the Agency for International Development and the National Endowment for Democracy. In 1988 the AFL-CIO budgeted $33 million on overseas activities—three times what it spent on organizing—of which $29 million came from U.S. government sources.[9] Funding has decreased in the 1990s but the U.S. government remains the AFL-CIO's main source of money for overseas activities. This is particularly ironic, since the AFL-CIO defines "free" labor unions with which it will cooperate as those which are not subject to government influence or control.

These AFL-CIO "internationalists" demanded that trade unionists shun all contact with unions tainted by communism. The "shunning" doctrine was carried so far that the AFL-CIO even withdrew from the ICFTU itself in the Vietnam War era to protest some European unions' contacts with communist-affiliated unions. Though it rejoined the ICFTU in 1982, the AFL-CIO's doctrine of "shunning" all unions affiliated with the WFTU was reaffirmed in 1985. In practice, the AFL-CIO often demanded that its affiliates shun not only communist unions, but even nonaligned unions that were members of neither world federation. This left the AFL-CIO virtually isolated from the rest of the world's labor movements, particularly with the newer movements of the Third World and the newly industrialized countries.

• Changing Labor Interests

For much of the Cold War era, the AFL-CIO's anti-communist internationalism could plausibly be portrayed as quite compatible with the short-term economic interests of U.S. trade unionists. "Foreign competition" was no threat to American workers because American industries dominated the markets of a war-devastated world. An expanding sphere of American military and ideological supremacy allowed American corporations to sell products abroad that could be produced only in war-spared America. Military expansion "primed the pump" at home while it secured the global "free market" for American products—to the apparent benefit of those who produced them.

Over the past two decades, a world dominated by U.S. corporations producing in the United States has been transformed into one dominated by global corporations producing all over the world. Allies like the United States, Germany, and Japan have become economic rivals. Military spending is increasingly perceived as a burden on national economies rather than as a source of prosperity. The disalignment of national security and economic interests is reflected in public attitudes: Most Americans now consider economic rivals like Japan the biggest threat to their national security.

During the 1980s, much of American labor responded to these trends by shifting from anti-communist internationalism to no internationalism. As international competition undermined U.S. economic hegemony, AFL-CIO policy switched from free trade to protectionism. Toyota-bashing became a Labor Day attraction and the employees of "foreign competitors" became objects of hate campaigns. Yet Toyota-bashing proved no more effective than smashing communist unions as a strategy for saving American jobs and preserving decent wages in a world of global corporations. Hence pressures increased at every level of the labor movement to develop an alternative.

- ## Labor in the Global Workplace

The pressures for change were intensified by the transformation in the world of work that accompanied the globalization of the economy.

The thirty years of economic growth following World War II that had brought prosperity to the industrialized world was based on the production of standardized consumer goods for stable national markets regulated by Keynesian policies. The predictability and stability of demand in national markets contributed to relative job security for a generation of workers employed in the core manufacturing industries.

For the (mostly) male workers in the core goods producing industries, the hallmarks of the post-war system included job security, good wages and benefits, fixed work rules, standard shifts and work assignments, and regular improvements in wages and working conditions through union negotiated agreements. Similar conditions existed for workers in the public sector.

Workers employed in the peripheral economy, in much of the service sector, those employed by smaller businesses, minority workers, and women did not, of course, fare so well. But even here the prevailing ideology of state activism made possible occasional wars on poverty (largely unsuccessful), new social service and entitlement programs, and basic civil rights legislation—all supported by the labor movement.

U.S. workers' protected position began to erode during the early 1970s. The emergence of Germany and Japan as economic powerhouses brought the era of U.S. global economic hegemony to an end, while the economic crisis of the early 1970s shook the post-war system to its core and marked the beginning of a restructuring of the global economy. The result has been the emergence of a new economic paradigm that continues to transform the global workplace. The sons and daughters of the post-war generation face declining living standards, economic uncertainty, and the further marginalization of those excluded from the core economy.

The mobility of capital in the new global economy has enabled corporations to organizationally outflank trade unions, which are rooted in national economies, by threatening to move operations abroad. Union strength is further undermined by persistent unemployment; the decline of employment among traditionally unionized industrial workers; sub-contracting and outsourcing, usually to small suppliers; the restructuring of traditional work practices, which often leads to downsizing; and the increase in part-time and temporary work. In some countries, such as the United States and Britain, hostile governments and restrictive labor laws have aided a corporate assault on union rights. Globalization requires that labor movements—whose strategies were rooted in nationally regulated economies—develop a global strategy.

The New Labor Internationalism

The breakdown of traditional labor strategies in the face of globalization, combined with the obsolescence of Cold War anticommunism, has begun to generate a new and quite different labor internationalism. This new internationalism began to crystallize in the late 1980s as a result of two related developments. First, labor activists' opposition to American involvement in Central America focused attention on AFL-CIO support for a U.S. foreign policy that encouraged the suppression of human and labor rights. Groups like the National Labor Committee for Human Rights in El Salvador struggled to change the AFL-CIO's position on Central America. They succeeded in legitimating for the first time real debate on what constitutes genuine international solidarity. Activists argued that the failure of the AFL-CIO to back progressive unions in Central America and elsewhere in the Third World cut off U.S. workers from contacts with such groups, leaving corporations free to play workers in different countries off against one another.

Second, a growing awareness of the consequences of economic globalization was highlighted by the growth of the maquiladoras of Mexico, where over 1,700 American and many Japanese companies built plants during the 1980s. For many on both sides of the border, the growth of the maquiladoras brought the changing nature of the world's economy right to their doorstep.

Many of these strands came together in the campaign against NAFTA, which represented a sea change for the American labor movement. It drew the official union bureaucracy into a fight which a few years before might have been restricted to a few dissidents. It broke the labor movement's reflex support for U.S. international policy. It showed that globalization was no longer seen to be in the interest of workers or their unions—posing though not answering the question of what the alternative might be. It demonstrated labor's ability, despite its oft-noted decline in power, to help mobilize a broad coalition concerned with the direction of the U.S. economy. And it showed that, despite its organizational rigidity, organized labor still has a social movement side, with rank and file networks that can draw workers and community allies into a struggle.

The new labor internationalism is developing a new set of strategies for international labor solidarity and a new infrastructure to support them. These include worker-to-worker exchanges, cross-border organizing, international labor rights, international strike support, and global labor communications. They form a prime example of the Lilliput Strategy of transnational cooperation to resist downward leveling.

- ### Worker-to-Worker Exchanges

Workers at the Ford truck plant in St. Paul, Minnesota remember the crisis a few years ago when the *Wall Street Journal* revealed that Ford was going to build an auto plant in Mexico. The Ford subcouncil of the UAW met and proposed to take any action necessary, even an immediate strike. Ford cooled out the protest by giving the UAW an ironclad promise that none of the cars would be imported into the United States. Soon Fords made in Mexico were everywhere and Ford workers began to look for a better way.

In 1990, St. Paul Ford workers learned that Marco Jimenez, a member of the Ford Workers Negotiating Committee in Cuautitlán Mexico, was touring the United States hoping to meet U.S. automobile workers to talk about common interests. Some of the St. Paul workers had heard about a strike at the Cuautitlán Ford plant near Mexico City in which nine workers had been shot, one fatally. They decided to invite Jimenez to visit their plant.

A flyer announcing the visit quoted a worker saying, "As long as Ford can treat people like slaves in one place, they will try to do it everywhere." The flyer also noted that "Local 879 bargainers have dealt with the same Ford negotiator, Tom Sterling, who negotiates for the Ford Motor Company in Mexico." Jimenez and local 879 recording secretary Tom Laney later wrote a joint article which described the meeting:

> When the two of us and other Ford workers met recently at the United Auto Workers local union hall in St. Paul, we agreed that we need to improve labor's international network for communication and mutual support. Our goal must be to push the companies and our governments to bring Mexican living and working conditions up towards U.S. levels, rather than allowing U.S. levels to be brought down.

The visit resulted in the St. Paul Local sending a delegation to the Cuautitlán plant and in the forging of lasting links between U.S. and Mexican Ford workers.

Such worker-to-worker exchanges have become an important way of building international solidarity. During the early 1990s an increasingly dense communication network developed in North America as organizations in the United States and Canada began sponsoring study tours to the maquiladoras of Mexico and inviting Mexican workers north. Organizations like the North American Worker-to-Worker Network (NAWWN), composed of representatives of labor and community groups around the continent, developed to promote contact and provide information on cross-border labor and community issues. NAWWN sponsors grassroots contact through tours and joint actions, publishes information and analysis of interest to North American workers, and helps promote cross border organizing campaigns. Detroit-based *Labor Notes* sponsors training sessions in Mexico for grassroots cross-border organizers.

Similar exchanges are organized worldwide by the Amsterdam-based Transnationals Information Exchange (TIE). It connects rank-and-file workers who work for the same global corporations and industries by means of study tours, conferences, seminars, and educational materials. TIE has branches in Europe, Asia, North America, and South America and transnational projects focused on the automobile, telecommunications, garment, and food processing industries.

- **Cross-Border Organizing**

The rise of the maquiladoras and the struggle over NAFTA have led to cross border alliances between U.S. unions and Mexican unions that are independent of the official, government-linked trade union federation. For instance, in 1994, St. Paul Ford workers expanded their ties to their Mexican counterparts by voting to pledge $300 a month—to come first from local union funds and then from rank-and-file pledges collected on the shop floor—to help support an organizer for the independent Mexican Authentic Workers' Front (FAT) union in the Ford Cuautitlán plant. Contributing members receive a jacket patch identifying them as "cross border solidarity organizers."[10]

The United Electrical workers, with support from the Teamsters, has entered a "strategic organizing alliance" with FAT to organize workers along the U.S.-Mexican border. The unions have targeted General Electric and Honeywell, companies where they currently represent workers in the United States.[11] Shortly after the passage of NAFTA, GE fired 11 Mexican workers in one plant and Honeywell fired 21 workers in another plant for trying to form independent unions. After international pressure, some though not all of the fired workers were rehired. The UE and Teamsters petitioned the newly created National Administrative Office of the Commission of Labor Cooperation, established under NAFTA's side agreements to deal with labor practices, thus setting up an early test of the Commission's effectiveness.[12]

- ## Labor Rights

Workers' rights groups like the ILRERF have kept a spotlight on labor rights abuses around the world, lobbied vigorously for passage and enforcement of U.S. laws limiting trade with countries denying basic labor rights, and worked closely with labor movements that face repression.

The National Labor Committee in Support of Worker and Human Rights in Central America—a coalition of 24 U.S. unions—has been active in the Central American and Caribbean regions in promoting labor rights and trade union organization, especially in the garment industry. The Labor Committee has been particularly successful in ending U.S. government-sponsored programs that encourage plants to relocate to Central America and the Caribbean region in order to take advantage of the suppression of unions.

- ## International Strike Support

International strike support has become an essential feature of major strikes in the global economy. For instance, one of the American labor movement's most impressive victories in recent years occurred at the Ravenswood Aluminum Corporation, which employs about 1,700 workers at its Ravenswood, West Virginia facility. In what *Business Week* described as "an unprecedented global campaign that's likely to be emulated by other labor groups," the U.S. Steelworkers "enlisted foreign unions" to force the employer's hand.[13]

In 1990 the company, formerly part of Kaiser Aluminum, was purchased by a three-person investment group, two of whom were based in Switzerland. One of the Swiss-based investors was Marc Rich, a fugitive from the United States, where he is wanted for tax evasion and fraud.

In 1990, after the sale, the new management locked out Ravenswood's workers during difficult contract talks and hired replacement workers. Steelworkers local 5668 launched an aggressive and ultimately successful 19 month campaign to defeat the lockout and win a decent contract. The campaign included strong rank-and-file participation to spread word of the strike around the country and to target end-users—those companies like Coca-Cola and Stroh's Brewing Company that used Ravenswood Aluminum in their cans.

Strong international pressure focused on Rich and his associates may have tipped the balance in favor of the workers. Under the direction of Joe Uehlein, Special Projects Director for the AFL-CIO's Industrial Union Department, a sophisticated campaign was developed to research Rich's holdings and embarrass him throughout the world. Uehlein credits strong support from the International Trade Secretariats and Swiss, Dutch, and Eastern European unions in applying pressure. The Steelworkers hired a full-time European coordinator for the campaign.[14] According to *Business Week*, the final victory came when "East European unions disrupted Rich's expansion efforts in Czechoslovakia, Romania, and Russia." Soon after, "a top Rich employee who owns most of Ravenswood's stock kicked out the aluminum producer's chairman and replaced him with another Rich associate. The company then agreed to restart contract talks with the union."[15]

When Caterpillar—the Illinois-based heavy equipment manufacturer long considered a global symbol of U.S. manufacturing know-how—demanded concessions from its workers during 1992 contract talks, it cited foreign competition, particularly from Japanese producers, as the reason. Management's demands precipitated a strike by 14,000 UAW members at Caterpillar.

After 5 months on strike, Caterpillar threatened to replace the strikers and reopen its plants. Workers in South Africa and Belgium staged sympathy strikes in support of U.S. workers. Caterpillar workers returned to work, conducted an intense in-plant campaign, and then struck again. They have also continued to build international support. In May, 1994 the International Metalworkers Federation held a conference of Caterpillar workers from around the world in Peoria, Illinois to discuss the situation at Caterpillar worldwide. UAW Secretary-Treasurer Bill Cas-stevens explained:

> Caterpillar likes to talk about "global competition"—a code word for corporate greed. We've got a better idea: global co-operation...While the company is hard at work trying to divide people, we're going to unite workers from different countries to discuss common problems, plan common strategies and work toward common solutions.[16]

Fifty trade unionists from eight countries set up an International Metalworkers Federation-Caterpillar network to exchange information about the company's anti-union activities. The International Metalworkers Federation will use the ILO to expose Caterpillar's violation of internationally accepted labor rights.[17]

- ## Global Labor Communications

Efforts to formalize communication among workers in global corporations have increased significantly. In the European Union, trade unions have been working to get a mandate from Brussels creating EU-wide Works Councils in multinational corporations. Some councils have already been organized. The European Trade Union Council has insisted that such councils—at least for the purposes of information exchange and consultation—are necessary to maintain effective representation in a borderless economy. While management is resisting mandated works councils, it is expected that some mechanism for transnational consultation in multinational firms will soon be mandated by the European Parliament.

Meanwhile, unions are reaching out across borders. The International Association of Machinists (IAM), representing workers at Northwest Airlines, has worked out an agreement to meet regularly to exchange information with its Dutch counterpart at KLM, which is a major shareholder in Northwest and shares its reservation system. The IAM has a similar agreement with the Transport General Workers Union (TGWU) at British Airways, which owns about a quarter of USAir.[18]

Computer networks are also emerging as an important element in the new labor internationalism. Computer conferences on the Institute for Global Communications' LaborNet provide instant information from around the world as well as forums for exchange of ideas. LaborNet also ties into other "Nets" dedicated to social movements like the environmental movement, peace movement, and human rights movement. Labor communications expert Peter Waterman has suggested that the increasing use of computers by labor and social movements constitutes a "communications internationalism," which he dubs a "Fifth International."[19]

Reconstructing the Labor Movement

Far from disappearing, the problems that the labor movement developed to address—first on a local and then on a national scale—are exacerbated by the global economy, which pits workers and communities against each other world-wide. Within the labor movement, there is a growing awareness that organized labor, as currently constituted, does not have either the strategy or the structures for the era of globalization. This is a crisis both for labor unions as organizations and for working people, who need a vehicle for collective action.

The challenges of globalization—unemployment, underemployment, changes in the nature of work, the decline of public services, and many others—are social issues that transcend the workplace. Meeting the challenge will require that the labor movement become a social movement that promotes the interests of all workers whether organized or unorganized. Trade unions must reach out of the workplace and into the community by building coalitions with environmental, community, religious, women's, human rights, farm, and other people's organizations. The Corporate Agenda pits workers and their communities against each other in a downward spiral which affects the vast majority of people. Ending that spiral requires developing an alternative agenda based on transnational organization of workers and allies to achieve upward leveling.

The anti-NAFTA campaign showed what it means for labor to play a central role in representing the economic interests of a broad spectrum of people. Here are some of the strategies for building on those initiatives:

- **Build New Forms of Representation at the Workplace**
Collective empowerment in the workplace is necessary to resist the race to the bottom—in the U.S. just as much as in the Third World. Yet most workers in the U.S. are deprived of the fundamental democratic right of workplace representation. Over 88 percent of all private sector workers are unorganized. Some projections have labor membership at 5 percent of the workforce by the year 2000.[20] At the present rate of organizing, if labor were to win every election it contested and sign a contract for every new bargaining unit, union membership would still decline.[21] One study estimates that to maintain present memberships, unions would have to spend $300 million dollars on organizing.[22]

Thomas Donahue, Treasurer of the AFL-CIO, observes that "new structures" may be needed to reverse labor's decline: "We have to look at this [the decline in membership] and ask, can we grow with the classic approach of the past, which is to organize workplace by workplace, employer by employer, signing up people one at a time. To make up for our losses and to get back to a position of real strength in the economy we will have to organize millions of workers. I am not sure you can do it one at a time."[23]

Creating new structures to represent workers will be a difficult task. Institutional inertia, hostile managements, and restrictive labor laws must be overcome. A free and open discussion at all levels of the labor movement and among other interested parties should begin immediately, and the issue of representation should be placed on the public agenda as a question of social rights in a democratic society. Forms of representation like German works councils, which are formally independent of the trade union movement, or the newly established Italian workers council system, which includes a formal union presence at the workplace, should be studied to see if they are adaptable to U.S. conditions.

On a transnational level, the European Union is developing regulations for transnational works councils for European-wide corporations. The councils would allow national unions to send representatives to a corporate-wide works council for information and consultation. Labor movements worldwide should find ways to build upon and expand this concept.

- ## Develop a New Workplace Agenda
  The adoption of lean production techniques and the growth of the contingent workforce are challenging labor movements around the world. Corporations seek to fill every minute of the work day and lay off workers when there is a drop in demand. Simple resistance to management's demand for "flexibility" is not an effective strategy in a highly competitive world and it puts the labor movement in the position of defending old fashioned "Taylorist" practices that were originally designed to intensify the exploitation of labor. Instead, the labor movement should engage the corporations with real, worker-designed workplace restructuring. This should include apprenticeship programs and continuous on-the-job training for multi-skilled jobs to help produce a genuinely flexible workforce. Real change must come from the bottom-up, driven by workers who have the hands-on experience with the system and the knowledge to transform it.

- ## Fight for Rights for All Workers
  A central labor movement goal should be a minimum package of rights for all workers, organized or unorganized, at the state and national level. This should include decent minimum wages, just cause for dismissals, effective plant closing rules, legally mandated vacations, health insurance, and other rights enjoyed by workers—organized or not—in most industrialized countries. The labor movement must develop ways to control the development of the contingent workforce by ensuring a full range of benefits and rights.

The instability of labor markets, characteristic of the global economy, means that unemployment will be a persistent problem. Unions should lead the fight for full employment policies at all levels of government and they should participate in grassroots community-based job creation initiatives. Unions must also lead the fight to organize unemployed workers and provide them an adequate social safety net.

- **Build Grassroots Internationalism**
Efforts to promote communication among rank-and-file workers and unions across borders should be expanded. Building links is a first step in a counter-offensive against the global corporate strategy. Organizations like NAWWN and TIE provide a good model for grassroots networking. Both local unions and Internationals should participate in cross-border organizing campaigns like those sponsored by the United Electrical Workers and Teamsters.

- **Reform AFL-CIO International Operations**
The AFL-CIO must break with its Cold War past. It should refuse U.S. government money for overseas activity. Its Foreign Affairs Department and regional institutes like AIFLD should be closed. The AFL-CIO should instead fund grassroots contacts by union members and local officials. This contact can encourage the development of a global awareness and the need for global solidarity. The Federation should open a dialogue with unions throughout the world regardless of political affiliation.

- **Make International Labor Rights a Top Priority**
At the top of labor's political agenda should be the inclusion of labor rights in U.S. trade policy and all international economic institutions. The fight for labor rights must also include the United States, where labor rights violations are a regular part of union organizing campaigns and one reason for low membership. Unions should continue to pursue and publicize U.S. labor rights violations in appropriate international venues.

- **Demand Ratification of ILO Conventions**

The United States has argued that U.S. law makes ratification of most ILO Conventions unconstitutional and has ratified only a handful of obscure conventions. Many legal experts think the legal arguments against ratification are dubious. The labor movement should make ratification a priority as an important first step in establishing some global standards to protect working people.

Without waiting for ratification, the AFL-CIO or a coalition of constituent unions should use the ILO Conventions to develop and promote a labor code for workers in the United States. Such a code, based on the ILO's international standards, could help bring worker rights in the United States up to the level of the rest of the industrialized world and help ensure that the United States is not demanding rights for workers in the developing world that do not exist in the United States.

- **Promote a North-South Labor/Social Movement Dialogue**

The labor movement should begin a dialogue with labor and social movements in the developing world to identify common interests and pursue a common agenda to counter downward leveling. One model is a series of joint seminars being held by Brazilian, Italian, and South African labor leaders.[24] It should take on as its own key Third World concerns, such as debt forgiveness and opposition to World Bank and IMF structural adjustment programs, which harm Third World peoples and at the same time accelerate the race to the bottom. The ICFTU's new "trade union strategy for world development" provides a starting point for this discussion.[25]

- **Reform the Institutions of Labor Internationalism**

Recently the ICTFU has begun to break with its Cold War past. The Brazilian movement CUT has joined and COSATU from South Africa may follow. Long time ICFTU observer (and critic) Peter Waterman comments that "The presence within the ICTFU of young, new, mass-mobilizing unions, linked with wider social movements in their societies, having some kind of socialist ideologies or aspirations, might renew the organization. They might also remind it of its origins in a 19th century emancipatory tradition of militant labor internationalism."[26] The ICFTU and its International Trade Secretariats (ITS) should expand their role in promoting rank-and-file interchange and developing transnational programs and strategies to counter the Corporate Agenda.

* * * * *

Such changes in the labor movement by themselves will not halt the race to the bottom. But, combined with similar changes in environmental, women's, religious, and other citizen groups all over the world, the impact could be enormous. An effective response to globalization starts with them.

Chapter
Nine

Reversing the Race to the Bottom

Globalization and the Corporate Agenda have engendered a new perspective or paradigm that we have called "globalization-from-below" and an approach to action we have called "the Lilliput Strategy." They are now generating an alternative global agenda—a Human Agenda to counter the Corporate Agenda.

This Human Agenda is emerging from common interests, shared pain, and evolving global norms of human rights, economic justice, and environmental sustainability. Such an Agenda is possible because globalization and the Corporate Agenda threaten such a wide range of human interests—and thereby create common interests among so many people. This is not to deny that conflicting interests remain important. But for most people in all parts of the world, a liveable future depends on reversing the race to the bottom.

A common human interest in protecting the global environment has come to be generally recognized: Ozone depletion and global warming are widely understood as threats to all.[1] We now need to recognize a similar common human interest in reversing the global economy's race to the bottom.

These common interests are not well represented in existing institutions—nation states, corporations, the UN, the IMF, World Bank, and GATT/WTO. So a Human Agenda corresponding to common human interests is more likely to emerge from a dialogue among social movements. The programs they produce[2] inevitably and properly express the common interests of specific coalitions. But they are also partial, often converging realizations of a Human Agenda integrating win-win approaches to the needs of people in rich and poor lands, environment and development, and different social and economic sectors.

There are certain criteria any proposed Human Agenda needs to meet:

- improve the lives of the great majority of the world's people over the long run

- correspond to wide common interests and integrate the interests of people in all parts of the world

- provide handles for action at a variety of levels

- include elements that can be at least partially implemented independently, but that are compatible or mutually reinforcing

- make it easier, not harder, to solve such non-economic problems as protection of the environment and reduction of war

- grow organically out of movements and coalitions that have developed in response to the needs of diverse peoples

In this chapter we present a program designed to reverse downward leveling. We have drawn heavily on proposals that have emerged from dialogue among social movements—particularly dialogues that cross national and issue boundaries. We have tried to put them together as a coherent alternative agenda, not just a laundry list of wished-for outcomes. We don't claim that this program represents "*the* Human Agenda"—only one possible approximation to be improved with discussion and tested in action.

Diverse Economic Philosophies

A few years ago, the greatest barrier to a common Human Agenda might well have been the "ideological" conflict of capitalism vs. communism. With the end of the Cold War, this highly oversimplified dichotomy has dissolved into a variety of alternatives that no longer necessarily take the form of choices between total systems.

Among those opposing downward leveling, there are few advocates for either an unregulated free market or a state command economy. But within these broad limits important differences in economic philosophy remain. There is no consensus on such questions as:

Should the future be based on an improved version of western industrial society or should human society move more in the direction of traditional indigenous cultures? Should local communities, regions, and countries be as economically self-reliant as possible, or should a wider economic interdependence be encouraged? Should growth continue to be a central economic objective, or should we instead pursue an economic steady-state? Should the lifestyle of the industrialized countries be maintained, or does it need to be transformed in order to allow development in poor countries without destroying the global environment? Should enterprises be owned and controlled by private individuals, by their workers, by communities, by states, or by some combination of these? What combination of market, state, and direct cooperation should organize economic life?

Different answers to such questions are not necessarily a barrier to cooperation in a broad movement against downward leveling, at least for the foreseeable future. Such a movement does not need complete unity on economic philosophy; rather, it should be a vehicle for debate and experimentation that helps test what works best for different circumstances and objectives.

There is also no reason that different groups and areas should not follow different "economic models" as long as they do so within a global framework that protects the environment, shares resources justly, and forestalls a race to the bottom. There may be nothing incompatible, for example, between some groups and/or regions following economic practices based on indigenous traditions and others pursuing ecologically corrected versions of Western industrial development.

Different practices, such as different degrees of economic integration, may also be appropriate in different sectors. For example, there are strong arguments for growing food close to where it will be consumed—from a reduced need for chemical preservatives to security against threats to food supply. Some of these arguments do not apply with as much force to manufactured goods, however—so decentralizing agriculture may be important while decentralized manufacturing may be less so.

Some very different approaches can even be incorporated as complementary, mutually supportive elements of a common program. For example, the funding of small-scale, grassroots-controlled, environment-enhancing cooperative activities based on indigenous models can both contribute to and gain support from global macroeconomic stimulus aiming to increase economic demand.

In the past, periods of economic reform have seen ferment in the discussion of economic alternatives. In the New Deal era, for example, various versions of labor and political organization, anti-monopoly policies, government regulation, socialism, communism, and communitarianism were hotly debated in schools, workplaces, unions, the press, and political organizations. Such an open discussion of alternative solutions should be a crucial part of today's global reconstruction.

Reconstructing the Global Economy from the Bottom Up

Downward leveling results from the extraction of wealth, power, and productive capacity from communities and the environment and their transfer to global corporations. A program for economic reconstruction needs to replace such downward leveling with upward leveling.

Upward leveling requires, first of all, empowering collective action. This means democratizing government at every level from the global to the local. Such democratization entails far more than simply periodic elections. It means, for example, eliminating the hold of wealthy contributors over election finance and the power of the IMF and World Bank over poor countries' economic policies. It means creating vehicles through which people can act on their common interests, such as local economic development programs. And it means holding corporations, banks, and other private economic actors accountable to the public, for example by means of enforceable corporate codes of conduct.

Second, upward leveling requires the transfer of resources—power, wealth, knowledge, organization—from haves to have-nots. This may be done in a great variety of ways, from protecting workers' right to organize to international commodity agreements stabilizing markets for Third World products.

Third, upward leveling requires ways to ensure that resources are used to meet the most important needs, not allowed to languish or be devoted to luxury and waste. That requires supporting global demand, cutting Third World debt, and increasing the purchasing power of those at the bottom. And it also requires redirecting resources from financial speculation and luxury cars to such pressing needs as the conversion to environmentally sustainable forms of production.

To pursue any one of the elements of this program by itself is no doubt difficult. But these elements are mutually reinforcing. For example, international cooperation of the kind proposed will allow national governments to channel investment to local communities without undermining their currencies or facing punishment from international financial institutions. Similarly, rising minimum wages will increase demand both for local producers and for the world market. The more these elements can be applied simultaneously, the easier and more effective they will be.

National institutions are not adequate for realizing this agenda, but neither would be a centralized global or a fragmented local system. Such a program has to be implemented at multiple levels. The decaying nation state-based economic system needs to evolve toward a multi-level, one-world economy in which public institutions regulate economic forces and allocate resources at multiple levels from local to global. These levels will no doubt include local, state/provincial, and national units in their historically evolved forms. They may also, however, include newly emerging formations, such as bio-regions and regional entities like the European Union. They may even involve non-territorial groups, such as ethnic or religious communities scattered across many lands. But however decentralized the system that emerges, it will not be able to prevent downward leveling if it does not have a global dimension.

Globalization has affected every economic structure from the World Bank to local governments and workplaces. Correcting its devastating impact will take changes in each of these interlocking structures. These changes do not all have to happen at once—like globalization itself, they are likely to break through at some points first, at others only later. People need to address their problems wherever they have power to do something about them—but in ways that support rather than undermine each other.

An Agenda for Upward Leveling

- Democratize

As long as democracy remains exclusively national it will remain largely powerless to address the economic problems of ordinary people. It will take democratization at each level from the local to the global to implement an effective alternative economic program. And it will take continuing grassroots mobilization to see that such a program actually works. Such democratization will require a struggle—but so has every advance in democracy from the American Revolution to the abolition of apartheid in South Africa. The democratic struggles of the past provide a treasury from which to draw and perfect means to use in the struggles of the future.

To cope with the New World Economy, the absolute version of national sovereignty must evolve toward a worldwide multilevel democracy. Global institutions like the World Bank, the IMF, and GATT/WTO will have to be radically democratized. Global corporations will have to be brought under democratic control. The global economy will have to be reshaped to encourage rather than impede democratic government at lower levels. National and local governments will have to be recaptured from the global corporations. They will have to support and cooperate with the environmental, economic, and social regulation that is needed at a global level—to serve as stewards representing global human and environmental interests in the areas under their control. People will have to win the right to organize in and democratically control their workplaces, schools, neighborhoods, and other institutions in civil society. In short, we need a multilevel process of democratization leading to democratic self-government at every level from the global to the local.

The demands of the Zapatistas in Mexico illustrate what it means for social movements to project democratization at multiple levels. They simultaneously demanded autonomous self-government for indigenous people in southern Mexico; free elections not dominated by wealth for Mexico as a whole; and an end to what they called the "neo-liberal project"[3] in Latin America.

In the New World Economy, democracy is not something we have; it is something we have to re-create. Democratization requires the redistribution of power. It currently has four principal fronts:

Democratize global institutions. The past decade has concentrated enormous power in such global institutions as the IMF,

World Bank, and GATT. Yet these institutions are virtually unaccountable to those who are affected by their decisions. Today, these organizations are dominated by the United States and a few other rich countries; their governance needs to be opened up to include the world's poor, represented by their governments and citizen organizations. Their operations are conducted with enormous secrecy; they need to be made open to public scrutiny. They are formally accountable only to national governments; they should be made more accountable to the United Nations and to non-governmental organizations representing citizen interests. They make decisions without the consent of local communities affected by them; their plans should be made in consultation with and require the approval of local communities they affect.[4]

End "preemption" of democratic decisionmaking. A principal function of global institutions and agreements has become to prevent governments from doing things their people want them to. The Uruguay Round GATT agreement, for example, restricts the freedom of countries to favor domestic suppliers, subsidize domestic businesses, impose health or environmental standards above specified levels, control prices, nationalize anything, or engage in economic planning. The effect of these restrictions is almost always to "preempt" governments from doing things that would raise labor, social, and environmental conditions.

Such negative "conditionalities" should be ended. Instead, international rules should encourage governments to improve the conditions of their people. Rather than punishing countries for spending on education, health, and welfare, the conditions governments and international institutions require for loans, investment, aid and trade advantages should encourage them. International standards should be "floors" not "ceilings."

Recapture governments from global corporations. All over the world, national, provincial, and local governments have become the pawns of global corporations and the Corporate Agenda. This has occurred through legal domination of the political process, political corruption, erosion of democratic processes, and the power of blackmail provided by capital mobility. Coalitions of popular movements and organizations, utilizing tactics adapted to the political context at hand, need to challenge this domination. People need to reassert the right to use governments to regulate corporations and markets in the public interest.

Establish the right to self-organization. Such basic human rights as freedom of speech, assembly, publication, political participation, unionization, cultural expression, and concerted action are crucial supports for resistance to downward leveling. Yet they are widely denied, not only in authoritarian governments, but also in workplaces, schools, and other institutions of supposedly democratic countries. Democratic organization in and control of such institutions can be a crucial vehicle for resisting downward leveling. The self-organization and empowerment of discriminated-against groups, such as racial and ethnic minorities, women, immigrants, and migrants is particularly crucial for countering the race to the bottom.

• Coordinate Global Demand

Ironically, as the economy has become more globalized, international cooperation to encourage adequate global economic demand has been virtually abandoned. The richer countries must share responsibility for countering the current downward spiral.

In the past, minimum labor standards, welfare state programs, collective bargaining, and other means to raise the purchasing power of have-nots did much to counter recessions and depressions within national economies. So did the tools of monetary and fiscal policy. Similar instruments increasing the buying power of those at the bottom and providing economic stimulus are now required in the global economy.[5]

Ending the world economy's downward spiral requires ad hoc, and eventually institutionalized, coordination. The IMF needs either to be replaced with a new agency or radically reformed in its purposes, policies, and personnel. Its goal should be to regulate the flow of capital, debt, and repayment to end the present downward economic spiral, reverse the polarization of wealth and poverty, and support the efforts of lower-level polities to mobilize and coordinate their economic resources.

Economist Walter Russell Mead has spelled out a possible institutional structure for such coordination. It includes an international fund to provide global economic stimulus; an international bank and specialized international agencies able to adjust interest rates and expand and contract their operations to promote growth and counter economic cycles; and an international trade organization devoted to encouraging the growth of global demand rather than the expansion of exports for their own sake.[6] The UN Development Program's *Human Development Report 1992* similarly calls for a new global central bank "to create a common currency, to maintain price and exchange-rate stability, to channel global surpluses and deficits, to equalize international access to credit—and to provide the liquidity and credits poor nations need."[7]

Expanded demand will primarily increase the consumption of the wealthiest unless it is combined with global redistribution. The International Confederation of Free Trade Unions has recently proposed a "trade union strategy for world development" that links coordinated recovery in the industrialized countries with jobs and poverty reduction in the developing world. It proposes expanded currency reserves for developing countries and Central and Eastern Europe; debt relief; and redesign of structural adjustment programs to emphasize reducing poverty and creating jobs. Such an approach provides a starting point for a "grand bargain" between North and South.[8]

- Establish Global Rights and Standards

To prevent competition among workforces and communities from resulting in a "race to the bottom," we need minimum global standards for human, labor, and environmental rights. The European Community's "Social Dimension" provides one possible model for minimum standards in such matters as job security, occupational safety, unemployment compensation, union representation, and social security benefits.[9] For North America, *A Just and Sustainable Trade and Development Initiative* spells out in some detail an alternative to NAFTA that would protect human and worker rights, encourage workers' income to rise in step with productivity, and establish continental environmental rights, such as the right to know about environmental threats and the right to a toxic-free workplace and living environment.[10] Such rights and standards need to be incorporated in a wide range of international economic agreements and institutions.

- **Enforce Codes of Conduct for Global Corporations**
  Global corporations should be made accountable by means of codes of conduct. Such codes might require corporations to report investment intentions; disclose hazardous materials imported; ban employment of children; forbid environmental discharge of pollutants; require advance notification and severance pay when operations are terminated; and require companies not to oppose union organization. While such codes should ultimately be enforced by the United Nations and by agreement among governments, global public pressure and cross-border organizing can begin to enforce them directly.

- **Reverse the Squeeze on the Global Poor**
  Globalization has been marked by the extraction of wealth from poor countries and communities. The richer countries have used international economic institutions to force a destructive flow of wealth from poor to rich. This is disastrous both for the people of the poor countries, for whom it has been a sentence of poverty and often premature death, and for those of the industrialized countries, who have lost markets for their products and had to face competition from impoverished workforces.

  The first step to reversing this process is to end the structural adjustment and shock therapy programs that the IMF and World Bank have been forcing on poor countries and countries emerging from state-run economies.

  Second, new arrangements should be made so that these countries do not have to run their economies to pay the interest on their debt. Debts for the poorest countries should be written off. Debts for other developing countries should be reduced, with the remaining parts paid in local currencies into a fund for local development.[11]

Third, large-scale resource transfers should be provided so that "developing" countries can in fact develop. Reformed trade rules can play a major role. The Third World Network proposes commodity agreements to improve and stabilize poor countries' terms of trade; opening rich country markets to poor countries; and preferential treatment for underdeveloped countries.[12] The Third World Information Network (TWIN) and other groups have developed strategies for alternative forms of trade which they are implementing on a small scale.[13] Under such conditions, trade can become a win-win proposition for different regions—for example, the production in the North of environmentally sound capital goods for the South, with production in the South of consumer goods for the North. Resource transfer also requires some direct compensatory funding; models for such funding can be drawn from the compensatory funds of the EU and the grass-roots funds of NGOs.

- **Encourage Grassroots Development**
  Deregulation and austerity policies have meant the drain of resources out of local communities. The forced opening of markets to global corporations has created conditions in which small local enterprises are unable to compete. We need instead to foster local, small-scale businesses and farms and a growing "third sector" of grassroots, community- and employee-owned cooperative enterprises designed to mobilize poorly utilized resources to address unmet needs. Here are some techniques for doing so.

  Grassroots-controlled enterprises. The last few years have seen an enormous range of experiments in new forms of employee- and community-controlled enterprises. Initiatives in poor communities in Brooklyn, N.Y. and Waterbury, Connecticut, for example, have established employee-owned home health aide companies which provide a needed service to local communities and jobs to a workforce made up primarily of women of color.[14] In Mali, a cooperative formed by a group of women in the 1970s in the small town of Markala became the nucleus for a Women and Development Program that spread to more than 30 village groups. The women conduct such income-generating activities as soapmaking, small animal raising, cloth dyeing, and raising vegetables; they also receive training in how to manage the coops.[15] Such efforts provide a way ordinary people in local communities can control and benefit from productive activity.

Public development authorities. Local, regional, and national development authorities can serve as a vehicle for a proactive economic strategy. A current model is the Steel Valley Authority, established by ten towns in the Pittsburgh area with the power to float bonds, own and manage enterprises, and use the power of eminent domain to save or re-open threatened companies.[16] Another example is the recently created Connecticut Community Economic Development Program. Created by the state government and jointly controlled by the government, representatives of poor communities, and private investors, it provides funding and technical assistance for private, public, and cooperative enterprises in poor communities. Its goals include creation of jobs and development of skills, particularly for people who are unemployed, underemployed, or receiving public assistance; community participation in decision-making; establishment of self-sustaining enterprises; improving the environment; promoting affirmative action, equal employment opportunities and minority-owned businesses; and coordination with environmental and economic planning.[17] The Greater London Enterprise Board —abolished by Margaret Thatcher—provides an even broader vision of what such institutions can do, helping restructure industries and providing support to enterprises based on their contribution to such social objectives as equalizing opportunity, empowering workers, and strengthening communities.[18]

Development banks and credit unions. Banks can be a crucial vehicle for gathering resources and connecting them with needs across time and space. Various forms of community-based and cooperative banking have developed in the Third World and in poor communities in the United States. For example, over the past few decades, as most banks collected deposits in poor and middle class communities and channelled them into unproductive speculative investment, Chicago's South Shore Bank reversed this process, dedicating its resources to rebuilding a poor, majority African-American neighborhood which had been cut off from credit by other area banks. By providing residential mortgages and small business loans and organizing initiatives in commercial development and housing rehabilitiation, South Shore financed and redeveloped the neighborhood's infrastructure and services, funding the renovation of nearly 30 percent of the neighborhood's apartments.[19]

Sweat equity and labor exchange. Sweat equity converts labor into a right to a share in the product. It lets people build houses and thereby acquire a share of their ownership or work in enterprises and thereby acquire a proportion of their stock. Labor exchange allows people with different needs and abilities to help each other. In the Great Depression, mutual aid organizations made it possible for unemployed carpenters to fix other people's houses in exchange for fish caught by fishers or firewood gathered by laborers. A modern equivalent, known as a "service credit" program, lets people work as volunteers in meeting community needs and receive for each hour of service a "service credit" which entitles them to one hour of service for themselves, their family, or organization from others in the program. Such programs allow people to make use of resources which the mainstream economy leaves to languish.

Community-based development organizations. Solving economic problems requires mobilization of diverse segments of the community. In many parts of the world, citizen-based organizations and coalitions are playing a crucial role in representing the needs and mobilizing the capabilities of grassroots people and organizations. Perhaps the most famous is the Mondragon network of banks, social service oganizations, technical education institutions, and producer cooperatives in the Basque region of Spain. In the United

States, several dozen citizen coalitions in different cities are grouped in the Federation for Industrial Retention and Renewal (FIRR). They mobilize community support to aid employee buyouts, start coops, pressure corporations and banks, and encourage government to support local economic development.[20]

- ### Rebuild the Public Sector

A central aspect of the Corporate Agenda has been to defame and dismantle those sectors of the economy private companies do not control. Structural adjustment programs and the desire to reduce business taxes have led to sharp cutbacks in public sector activities all over the world. The constant attack on government and the privatization of formerly public functions has led to worldwide decay of education, healthcare, infrastructures, environmental protection and enhancement, and services for the young, the old, and the disabled. It has also led to unemployment and aggravation of the downward spiral.

The "free market" has proved an inadequate vehicle for performing many such functions. Even where large numbers of people are unemployed and other resources lie idle, markets do not necessarily channel them to meeting such public needs. An expansion of education, health, infrastructure, environmental, and similar public sector activities is an essential element of economic reconstruction.[21]

- ### Convert to Sustainable Production and Consumption

The victims of downward leveling need, want, and deserve a better life. But the current industrial system is already destroying the earth's air, water, land, and biosphere. Global warming, desertification, pollution, and resource exhaustion will make the earth uninhabitable long before every Chinese has a private car and every American a private boat or plane.

The solution to this dilemma lies in converting the system of production and consumption to an ecologically sound basis. The technology to do this exists or can be developed, from solar energy to public transportation and from reusable products to resource-minimizing production processes. However, a system in which the search for ever-expanding profits has no regulation or limits will continue to use environmentally destructive processes to produce luxuries, pollutants, and waste.

This malappropriation of resources is exacerbated by the huge share of human wealth squandered on the military. Despite the end of the Cold War, global military spending is more than $1,000 trillion per year—nearly half of it by the United States.[22] This is justified in large part by the need to control economic rivals and the revolts of poor and desperate peoples.

The energies now directed to the race to the bottom need to be redirected to rebuilding the global economy on a humanly and environmentally sound basis. Such an approach requires limits to growth—in some spheres, sharp reductions—in the material demands that human society places on the environment. It requires reduced energy and resource use; less toxic production and products; shorter individual worktime; and less production for war. But it requires vast growth in education, health care, human caring, recycling, rebuilding an ecologically sound production and consumption system, and time available for self-development, community life, and democratic participation.

* * * * *

The vehicle for realizing the Human Agenda is not something that pre-exists; it is a social movement under construction. Those who seek to realize their own interests by working with others to advance the common human interest are part of it. To correct David Rockefeller's refrain, "Broad human interests" are "being served best" when *human cooperation* is "able to transcend national boundaries."

Notes

Notes to Introduction—2nd Edition

1. Roger Cohen, "Argentine Economy Reborn but Still Ailing," *The New York Times*, February 6, 1998, p. A1.

2. John Cavanagh and Sarah Anderson, "The Impact of Capital Flows on Workers in the Global Economy," March 1, 1998, Institute for Policy Studies; "Toward a New Financial System," *The Economist*, April 11, 1998.

3. John Tagliabue, "For Americans, an Indirect Route to the Party," *The New York Times*, June 14, 1998, p. 3: 4, citing James E. Carlson, economist at Merrill Lynch in New York.

4. *International Herald Tribune*, January 15, 1998.

5. John J. Sweeney, "Making the Global Economy Work for America," Economic Strategy Institute Conference, May 5, 1998, citing *Business Week* (http://www.aflcio.org/publ/speech98/sp0505.htm).

6. "Emergency Response Network to Intensify Sweatshop Fight," *Labor Notes*, June 1998, p. 9.

7. Video interview.

8. Sam Dillon, "Aeromexico Strike Marks Transition," *The New York Times*, June 8, 1998, p. A6, citing Sidney Weintraub, economist at Georgetown University's Center for Strategic and International Studies.

9. Fareed Zakaria, "Will Asia Turn Against the West?" Op-Ed, *The New York Times*, July 10, 1998, p. A15.

10. Uli Schmetzer, "25% of Russians Are Living Below Subsistence Level, Official Says," *Chicago Tribune*, October 15, 1996, p. 8, citing First Deputy Prime Minister Viktor Ilyushin.

11. Bruce F. Pauley, "Edge of Poverty Sharper for Many Russians Today," *Orlando Sentinel*, September 29, 1996, p. G1.

12. Lester Thurow, cited in "Wages or Wealth?" *Center Focus*, December 1997, Center of Concern, Washington, D.C.

13. Robert Reich, "Broken Faith: Why We Need to Renew the Social Compact," *The Nation*, February 16, 1998 (http://www.thenation.com/issue/980216/ 0216reic.htm).

14. Jeff Madrick, "Computers: Waiting for the Revolution," *New York Review of Books*, March 26, 1998, p. 30.

15. William Greider, "When Optimism Meets Overcapacity," Op-Ed, *The New York Times*, October 1, 1997, p. A27.

16. *New York Times*, April 5, 1998.

17. Sweeney, "Making the Global Economy Work for America," citing *Business Week*, April 20, 1998.

18. "Colloquy: Global Roulette: In a Volatile World Economy, Can Everone Lose?" *Harper's Magazine*, June 1998, p. 39.
19. David E. Sanger, "Asia's Economic Tigers Growl at World Monetary Conference," *The New York Times*, September 22, 1997, p. A1.
20. Cohen, "Argentine Economy Reborn but Still Ailing," p. A1.
21. Kim Moody, "Workers in a Lean World," a speech to the Brecht Forum in New York, New York, November 14, 1997. Broadcast on Alternative Radio (ar@orci.com).
22. Jeremy Brecher, *Strike!: Revised and Updated Edition* (Boston: South End Press Classics, 1997), p. 4.
23. Social and economic alternatives forum, draft document available in English and Spanish on the Summit of the Peoples of the Americas web page (http://members.tripod.com/~redchile/introe.htm).
24. John Russo and Andrew Banks, "Building Global Trade Union Campaigns and Organizing Structures: Taking the UPS Strike Overseas," presented at the UCLEA/AFL-CIO Education Department Conference, "Organizing for Keeps," San Jose, California, May 2, 1998.
25. Brecher, *Strike!* pp. 352-53.
26. Sweeney, "Making the Global Economy Work for America."
27. Peter Sutherland and John Sewell,"Viewpoint: Gather the Nations To Promote Globalization," *The New York Times*, February 8, 1998, p. 3: 15.

Notes to Introduction

1. According to the *Boston Globe*, "Corporate taxes are crumbling in many industrial countries as companies move their booked profits from one locale to another, telling different stories to different tax collectors." The General Accounting Office told Congress in 1993 that 40 percent of corporations with assets of at least $250 million paid less than $100,000 in U.S. income taxes. *Boston Globe*, April 11, 1994.
2. For international perspectives on the broader aspects of globalization, see Jeremy Brecher, John Brown Childs, and Jill Cutler, eds., *Global Visions: Beyond the New World Order* (Boston: South End Press, 1993).
3. Statement of subcomandante Marcos, quoted in *Inter-American Trade Monitor*, vol. 3, no. 2, January 10, 1994.
4. *The New York Times*, March 24, 1994.
5. Martin Khor, "500,000 Indian farmers rally against GATT and patenting of seeds," *Third World Resurgence*, No. 39, November 1993. "Satyagraha" is the term Mahatma Gandhi used for the nonviolent civil disobedience movements he led.
6. David Peterson, "The New Solidarity," *Z*, February 1994, p. 9.
7. "Poles Hold March Over New Budget," *The New York Times*, February 10, 1994.

8. *The New York Times*, April 3, 1993.

9. As far as we know, the term "globalization-from-below" was first used by Richard Falk in "The Making of Global Citizenship" in *Global Visions*.

10. In a series of meetings over the past two years, for example, representatives from environmental, labor, religious, consumer, and farm groups from Mexico, the United States, and Canada have prepared *A Just and Sustainable Trade and Development Initiative for North America*. (Alliance for Responsible Trade, Citizens Trade Campaign, Mexican Action Network on Free Trade, and Action Canada Network, 1994): Two conferences and a series of follow-up discussions sponsored by the American Friends Service Committee have produced a parallel proposal, "From Global Pillage to Global Village: A Perspective from Working People and People of Color on the Unregulated Internationalization of the Economy and the North American Free Trade Agreement," which has been endorsed by over sixty grassroots organizations (Philadelphia: American Friends Service Committee, 1994). Similar proposals by the Third World Network have recently been published as "Toward a New North-South Economic Dialogue" in *Third World Resurgence*, August 1993, pp. 18-21.

11. Jeremy Brecher and Tim Costello, *Common Sense for Hard Times* (Boston and Washington, D.C.: South End Press and Institute for Policy Studies, 1976).

12. For some examples see *Building Bridges: The Emerging Grassroots Coalition of Labor and Community*, edited by Jeremy Brecher and Tim Costello (New York: Monthly Review Press, 1990).

Notes to Chapter One
The Race to the Bottom

1. "Multinationals Under Siege," *International Finance*, May 19, 1975. Cited in Holly Sklar, ed. *Trilateralism: The Trilateral Commission and Elite Planning for World Management* (Boston: South End Press, 1980).

2. Gary Clyde Hufbauer et. al., "The Case for Free Trade" in *The Free Trade Debate*, edited by Twentieth Century Fund, Task Force on the Future of American Trade Policy (New York: Priority Press Publications, 1989), p. 8.

3. *The Boston Globe*, July 10, 1994.

4. MIT economist Paul Krugman has written, "If there were an Economist's Creed it would surely contain the affirmations, 'I believe in the Principle of Comparative Advantage,' and 'I believe in free trade.'" Paul Krugman, "Is Free Trade Passé?" *Economic Perspectives* 1, no. 2. Cited in Daly, Herman E. and John B. Cobb, Jr., *For the Common Good* (Boston: Beacon Press, 1994), p. 209.

5. *The New York Times*, June 23, 1992; *Financial World*, May 24, 1994, p. 26.

6. Ken Coates, "Social Dumping Won't Work," *Chartist*, July-August, 1993.

7. *The New York Times*, April 20, 1994.

8. Richard J. Barnet and John Cavanagh, "Just Undo It: Nike's Exploited Workers," *The New York Times*, February 13, 1994.

9. *The New York Times*, March 17, 1994.

10. Robert B. Reich, *The Work of Nations*, (New York: Vintage Press, 1992), p. 8. Some critics have questioned the reality and/or importance of economic globalization, or at least the extreme version of it proposed by Reich. Laura D'Andrea Tyson, now chair of President Clinton's Council of Economic Advisors, for example, pointed out in 1991 that Japanese, German, and U.S.-owned companies still produce the lion's share of their output in their home countries. ("They Are Not Us: Why American Ownership Still Matters," *American Prospect*, Winter 1991.) Economist Timothy Koechlin of Skidmore College argues that "The evidence indicates that there continues to be a strong link between the nation state and the process of capital accumulation, suggesting that sweeping assertions about the 'globalization of capital' provide a poor basis for understanding both the process of capital accumulation and its implications for workers and others." ("The Globalization of Investment: A Critical Perspective," unpublished paper.) But even these critics of strong versions of the "globalization" thesis acknowledge the underlying dynamic of the race to the bottom. Tyson recently observed that "Globalization has depressed the wage growth of low wage workers." (*The New York Times*, July 10, 1993.) Koechlin writes "International investment is extremely significant in some industries and, further, a little capital mobility may go a long way toward limiting the aspirations of workers and reform minded policy makers." Indeed, he argues that NAFTA "is likely to undermine living standards of US workers precisely because it enhances the viability of the threat of relocation." (Koechlin, "The Globalization of Investment.")

11. Richard J. Barnet and John Cavanagh, *Global Dreams* (New York: Simon and Schuster, 1994), p. 15.

12. Stephen Viederman, "Ecological Literacy," text of keynote address to the Associated Colleges of the Midwest Conference on Ecological Education, March 11, 1994.

13. *The New York Times*, May 21, 1989.

14. For case studies of global corporations, see Barnet and Cavanagh, *Global Dreams*. For further analysis, see Bennett Harrison, *Lean and Mean: The Changing Landscape of Corporate Power in the Age of Flexibility* (New York: Basic Books, 1994).

15. Robert Reich, *The Work of Nations* (New York: Vintage, 1992), p. 113.

16. John Gerard Ruggie, "Territoriality and Beyond," *International Organization*, vol. 47, no. 1, winter 1993, p. 141.

17. Saskia Sassen, "Economic Globalization: A New Geography, Composition, and Institutional Framework," *Global Visions: Beyond the New World*

Order, edited by Jeremy Brecher, John Brown Childs, and Jill Cutler (Boston: South End Press, 1993), p. 62-63.

18. Judy Shelton, quoted in *The New York Times,* May 8, 1994.

19. For further discussion of these wider aspects of globalization, see *Global Visions.* "Globalization" does not imply a uniform development throughout the world or for all sectors of the economy. For example, the era of globalization has had profoundly different impacts in Africa and in East Asia. For an analysis of economic globalization by geography, composition, and institutional framework, see Sassen in *Global Visions.*

20. *The New York Times,* March 17, 1994.

21. Michael T. Donaghu and Richard Barff, "NIKE Just Did It: International Subcontracting and Flexibility in Athletic Footwear Production," *Regional Studies,* vol. 24, December 1990, p. 545, quoted in Harrison, *Lean and Mean,* p. 207.

22. *The Boston Globe,* July 10, 1994.

23. Dan Gallin, "Drawing the Battle Lines," *New Politics,* summer 1994, pp. 109-110.

24. *The New York Times,* March 22, 1994.

25. *The New York Times,* October 13, 1987.

26. Lawrence Mishel and Jared Bernstein, *The State of Working America: 1992-93* (Armonk, NY: M.E. Sharpe, 1993).

27. *The New York Times,* February 11, 1994. The modest but widely touted reduction in the male/female wage gap is due primarily to men's wages falling—not to women's wages rising.

28. *The New York Times,* May 30, 1994.

29. *Financial Times,* September 3, 1993, quoted in Denis MacShane, "Economic Interdependence—New Policy Challenges," paper prepared for submission to European Parliament hearing, Brussels, September 28, 1993, p. 5.

30. Clayton S. Collins, "Temptation Costs Jobs," *Union Plus,* Spring 1994.

31. *The New York Times,* March 10, 1994. One worker who worked two jobs and whose wife worked two jobs, informed of recent statistics on job growth, commented "Sure, we've got four of them. So what. So you can work like a dog for $5 an hour." (*The New York Times,* March 11, 1994.)

32. "Teamsters' Extra Load," *The Boston Globe,* April 25, 1994.

33. *The New York Times,* March 13, 1994.

34. Juliet Schor, *The Overworked American* (New York: Basic Books, 1991), p.29. See also Jeremy Brecher and Tim Costello, "The Great Time Squeeze," Z, October 1990.

35. Study cited in Harrison, *Lean and Mean,* p. 205.

36. U.N. Human Development Program, *Human Development Report* (New York: Oxford, 1993), p. 12.

37. *The Boston Globe,* July 10, 1994.

38. See for example Walden Bello, *Dragons in Distress: Asia's Miracle Economies in Crisis* (London: Penguin, 1991) and Chee Yoke Ling, "The environmental and social cost of South-east Asia's economic success," *Third World Resurgence*, no. 42/43, February/March 1994.

39. *The New York Times*, July 5, 1994.

40. Robin Broad with John Cavanagh, *Plundering Paradise: The Struggle for the Environment in the Philippines* (Berkeley and Los Angeles: University of California Press, 1993), pp. 31-32.

41. *The New York Times*, March 11, 1994.

42. Data from U.S. Bureau of Labor Statistics, cited in *AFL-CIO News*, December 13, 1993.

43. *The New York Times*, March 22, 1994. Downsizing and job loss of course result in substantial part from an increase in productivity resulting from the introduction of new technology. Such productivity growth is a normal feature of capitalist economies. Under some conditions such productivity growth can lead to stable or even increasing employment. Globalization is currently undermining those conditions, however. Current U.S. corporate investment is focused on lowering costs by replacing existing equipment rather than on expanding production. As David Wyss, chief economist at DRI/McGraw Hill put it, "American companies, being very cost-sensitive, are really trying to substitute machinery for labor rather than purchase more machinery and more labor. Why expand here if you know there is a company in Japan operating at only two-thirds of capacity and seeking business in America to fill up its shop. Or if there are skilled workers in Mexico who can do the job." Quoted in *The New York Times*, June 16, 1994.

44. *The New York Times*, March 10, 1994.

45. *Business Week*, May 9, 1994, p. 61.

46. *The New York Times*, May 6, 1994.

47. *The New York Times*, March 10, 1994.

48. With official unemployment at 6.5 percent early in 1994, Martin Feldstein of Harvard University, head of the National Bureau of Economic Research, stated, "We are essentially at full employment today." (*The New York Times*, March 28, 1994.) (Official unemployment figures do not include such groups as "discouraged workers" who have given up even looking for work and those working part-time who would prefer to work full-time.) Many economists regard unemployment at such levels as necessary to prevent inflation. According to William Dudley, a senior economist at Goldman, Sachs & Company, "We are in fact approaching a level of full employment and capacity utilization that would represent a point at which the inflation rate could be expected to climb." (ibid.) Labor Secretary Robert B. Reich commented on the use of mass unemployment to reduce inflation, "If it is true that we have to draft seven to

eight million people into unemployment in order to fight inflation, then we have a major social problem on our hands." (ibid.)

49. *The New York Times*, March 10, 1994.

50. The Japanese Employers Federation estimates that Japan's unemployment rate would rise from 3 percent to 5 or 6 percent if Japanese employers cut "unneeded" jobs the way western firms do. (*The New York Times*, March 14, 1994.) Russia experienced a staggering 26 percent drop in production in 1993; according to President Boris Yeltsin, 20 percent of Russians live below the poverty line and 25 percent more are on the brink of destitution (*The New York Times*, June 11, 1994).

51. Bruce Rich, "World Bank/IMF: 50 Years Is Enough," in *50 Years Is Enough*, Kevin Danaher, ed. (Boston: South End Press, 1994), p. 13.

52. Nicholas Eberstadt, "Marx and Mortality: A Mystery," op ed, in *The New York Times*, April 6, 1994.

53. Samuel Morley, "Structural Adjustment and the Determinants of Poverty in Latin America," Occasional paper, Vanderbilt University and the Inter-American Development Bank, Washington, D.C., July 1992.

54. Walden Bello, "Global Economic Counterrevolution," in *50 Years Is Enough*, p. 18.

55. United Nations Economic Commission for Africa data, cited by Davison Budhoo,"IMF/World Bank Wreak Havoc on Third World," *50 Years Is Enough*, p. 21.

56. Quoted in Bello, *50 Years Is Enough*, p. 18.

57. Peter A. Vance, letter to the editor, *The New York Times*, February 28, 1994.

58. "Facing Up to Global Joblessness," *The New York Times*, July 10, 1993.

59. David C. Ranney and William Cecil, "Transnational Investment and Job Loss in Chicago: Impacts on Women, African-Americans and Latinos" (Chicago: University of Illinois at Chicago Center for Urban Economic Development, January 1993).

60. Hugh B. Price, president and CEO, National Urban League, keynote address to National Urban League Convention, Indianapolis, Indiana, July 24, 1994.

61. Kevin Philips, *The Politics of Rich and Poor* (New York: Harper Perennial 1991), p. xi.

62. Philips, p. xii.

63. Philips, p. xi.

64. *The New York Times*, April 12, 1994.

65. *The State of Working America: 1992-93*, p. 7.

66. U.N. Human Development Program, *Human Development Report 1992*, pp. 36ff.

67. Susan George, "The Debt Boomerang," in *50 Years Is Enough*, p. 29.

68. Susan George, "The Debt Boomerang," in *50 Years Is Enough*, p. 30.

69. Walter Wriston, "The Decline of the Central Bankers," op ed, *The New York Times*, September 20, 1992.

70. *The New York Times*, May 8, 1994. Economist Peter Dorman notes that, in addition to the real constraints globalization places on national policy, there is also what he dubs "surplus neo-liberalism"—an unnecessary constraint resulting from an exaggerated belief in the power or wisdom of the global market.

71. *The New York Times*, June 20, 1994.

72. *The New York Times*, May 21, 1989.

73. Quoted in "Is Capitalism Doomed?" op ed by Benjamin C. Schwarz, *The New York Times*, May 23, 1994.

74. Many of the effects of "downward leveling" were predictable a decade ago; many were in fact predicted. See, for example, Jeremy Brecher, "Crisis Economy: Born-Again Labor Movement?" in *Monthly Review*, March, 1984.

75. *Boston Globe*, April 11, 1994, citing figures from the April 25, 1994 issue of *Forbes*. By the beginning of 1994, inflation-adjusted profits of U.S. corporations were close to an all-time high. (*The New York Times*, February 27, 1994.)

76. Sarah Anderson and John Cavanagh, "Workers Lose, CEOs Win: An Analysis of Executive Salaries at Top Job-Cutting Firms," press briefing paper (Washington, D.C.: Institute for Policy Studies), April 29, 1994. Based on *Forbes 500* figures released in April 1994 and *Business Week's* April 1994 survey of executive pay.

Notes to Chapter Two
The Era of Nation-Based Economies

1. The following historical discussion draws on Jeremy Brecher, "The 'National Question' Reconsidered," *New Politics*, Summer 1987. For the rise of the state see Quentin Skinner, *The Foundations of Modern Political Thought* (Cambridge: Cambridge University Press, 1978). For a pioneering effort to understand the significance of globalization for the theory of the state, see John Gerard Ruggie, "Territoriality and Beyond: Problematizing modernity in international relations," *International Organization*, vol. 47, no. 1, winter 1993. Our approach to all these questions has been influenced by Michael Mann, *The Sources of Social Power: Volume I: A history of power from the beginning to A.D. 1760* (Cambridge: Cambridge University Press, 1986); and Mann, *The Sources of Social Power: Volume II: The rise of classes and nation-states, 1760-1914*, (Cambridge: Cambridge University Press, 1993).

2. Ruggie, "Territoriality and Beyond," p. 149.

3. This system is sometimes referred to as the "Westphalian Model" after the Peace of Westphalia of 1648 which incorporated some of its principles.

4. Mann, Volume I, p. 513. Mann points out that "nothing in the capitalist mode of production" leads of itself to the emergence of "many networks of production, divided and at war, and of an overall class structure that is nationally segmental." (p. 515) To grasp what is novel about today's globalization it is necessary to see that it is emerging from a system that was both capitalist and national. See the two volumes of *The Sources of Social Power* for a recap of the extensive debates on the relation of states to capitalism and a defense of the impossibility of reducing either to the other.

5. This doctrine was an extension of these economists' celebration of the "invisible hand" of the market domestically. In much of the world this doctrine is known as "liberalism" and its recent revival as "neo-liberalism." In the United States, to make matters more confusing, "liberalism" generally refers to almost the opposite: an active role for the state in pursuit of public goals.

6. Alexander Hamilton, *Report on Manufactures*, December 5, 1791.

7. Quoted in William Appleman Williams, *The Contours of American History* (Cleveland and New York: World, 1961), p. 346.

8. Explanations for this observable reality vary. Keynes found the origin of equilibrium at less than full employment in "inadequate demand" caused by "liquidity preference"—the desire of wealth-holders not to invest based on the expectation of better gains from waiting than from investing. Marx also found the possibility of disaccumulation to originate in the ability of capitalists to sell without buying: an interruption of the circuit "commodities-money-commodities." However, for Marx it was the absence of an adequate overall regulator of the capital-labor relationship (other than the class struggle itself) which led capitalism to produce periodic economic crises and a chronic "relative surplus population" or "reserve army of labor." The system's regulator, the accumulation of capital by private firms, did not dictate full employment, particularly under conditions of changing labor productivity. Both Keynesian and Marxist theory allowed for the possibility that social resources and social needs might not be translated into economic supply and economic demand, and that resources might not be used to meet needs. Much contemporary economics, in contrast, assumes (in the tradition of Say's Law) that full employment is an automatic feature of a market system. Such theories have the splendid virtue of making mass involuntary unemployment impossible.

9. For recent scholarship on the New Deal, see Steve Fraser and Gary Gerstle, ed., *The Rise and Fall of the New Deal Order, 1930-1980* (Princeton: Princeton University Press, 1989).

10. In the early 1970s, U.S. Republican President Richard Nixon proclaimed, "We are all Keynesians now."

11. It has been referred to by various other names as well, such as corporate liberalism, Fordism, and the Keynesian order.

Notes to Chapter Three
The Dynamics of Globalization

1. Profit rate defined as net operating surplus divided by net capital stock at current prices. Andrew Glyn, Andrew Hughes, Alain Lipietz, and Agit Singh, "The Rise and Fall of the Golden Age," in *The End of the Golden Age,* Stephen Marglin and Juliet Schor, eds. (New York: Oxford University Press, 1989), pp. 39-125, cited in Bennett Harrison, *Lean and Mean: The Changing Landscape of Corporate Power in the Age of Flexibility* (New York: Basic Books, 1994), pp. 125-126.

2. *The New York Review of Books,* June 25, 1987, p. 32.

3. It also no doubt reflects less structural factors, such as the temporary formation of an international oil cartel and the brief but highly disruptive "oil shocks" it caused.

4. Quoted in Chakravarthi Raghavan, *Recolonization: GATT, Uruguay Round and the Third World* (Penang: Third World Network, 1990), p. 55.

5. Quoted in Howard Wachtel, *Money Mandarins: The Making of a New Supranational Economic Order* (New York: Pantheon, 1986), p. 137.

6. David C. Ranney, *The Evolving Supra-National Policy Arena* (Chicago: University of Illinois at Chicago, Center for Urban Economic Development, 1993). This "destruction of claims on value" could also be considered a means by which firms "externalize" such costs as environmental depletion and destruction, maintaining the health of the workforce, and raising and educating the next generation of workers.

7. Saskia Sassen,"Economic Globalization: A New Geography, Composition, and Institutional Framework," in Jeremy Brecher, John Brown Childs, and Jill Cutler, eds., *Global Visions: Beyond the New World Order* (Boston: South End Press, 1993), p. 62.

8. "Stateless monies: A new face in world economics," *Business Week,* August 21, 1978, p. 78, quoted in Ranney, *Policy Arena,* p. 13.

9. Felix Rohatyn, "World Capital: The Need and the Risks," *The New York Review of Books,* July 14, 1994, p. 48-49.

10. Steven Rattner, "Europe Can't Heal Britain's Economy," op ed, *The New York Times,* December 9, 1990. Some have argued that globalization does not prevent the use of Keynesian policies at a national level. To defend this position they need to address these and other similar examples. Of course, in a global economy with unused capacity, stimulation of a national economy may expand imports without bidding up prices and thereby cause inflation. But the stimulus may still cause foreign rather than domestic growth.

11. Harrison, *Lean and Mean,* p. 127.

12. Harrison, pp. 9, 171.

13. Harrison, p. 12. Herman Daly has predicted that "ten years from now the buzz words will be 'renationalization of capital.'" ("Farewell Lecture

to the World Bank." Quoted in Donella Meadows, "Listen to Herman Daly," *Why?*, Summer 1994, p. 13.) How this will happen, given the advantages possessed by corporations with global reach, is not evident.

14. Harrison, pp. 9-10.

15. Harrison, p. 190.

16. Harrison, p. 12.

17. We use the term "agenda" to refer to an open-ended plan—one which outlines a set of intentions but presumes that they will be subject to additional input. It refers in effect to the conscious, purposeful, planned element of social development, as contrasted to "process" or "drift."

18. Of course, these policies were not always what they purported to be. First World financial institutions and banks, for example, eagerly encouraged Third World countries to take on mountains of debt—leading to a continuing crisis of unrepayable debt. The Reagan administration, while excoriating Keynesian economics in the name of balanced budgets, simultaneously cut taxes on the wealthy and doubled the military budget. This provoked unprecedented budget deficits and helped turn the United States from the world's largest creditor to its largest debtor in a single decade.

19. See Thomas Ferguson and Joel Rogers, *The Hidden Election: Politics and Economics in the 1980 Presidential Campaign*, (New York: Pantheon Books, 1981).

20. This discussion of the global policy arena draws on Ranney's *The Evolving Supra-National Policy Arena*, which provides many of the relevant details and references.

21. Ranney, p. 24.

22. Walden Bello, *Dark Victory* (Oakland, Calif.: Food First, 1994), p. 27.

23. These polices were often touted as a way to turn underdeveloped countries into "NICs." However, the most successful NICs, such as Korea, Taiwan, and earlier Japan, in fact had highly regulated and protected national economies. Repeating the early NICs' success was also far more difficult for latecomers to the largely saturated global market.

24. *Wall Street Journal*, May 9, 1994.

25. Ibid.

26. *Trade Liberalisation: Global Economic Implications*, cited in Martin Khor Kok Peng, "The End of the Uruguay Round and Third World Interests" (Penang: Third World Network, February 1994.)

27. *The New York Times*, April 14, 1994.

28. Testimony of Ralph Nader before the Trade Subcommittee of the House Ways and Means Committee, February 2, 1994.

29. Charles W. Thurston, "Regional Blocs Work to Expand Trade, Analysts Say," *Journal of Commerce*, May 23, 1994. See also Beth V. Yarbrough and Robert M. Yarbrough, "Regionalism and Layered Governance: The

Choice of Trade Institutions," *Journal of International Affairs*, Spring 1994, Vol. 48, No.1.

30. For further discussion of this subject, see Jeremy Brecher's "The Hierarchs' New World Order—And Ours" in *Global Visions*.

31. The phrase is from Colombian diplomat Luis Fernando Jaramillo, chairman of the Group of 77. Cited in Martin Khor Kok Peng, "The End of the Uruguay Round and Third World Interests."

32. National and U.N. military operations have increasingly been justified as vehicles for maintaining a "New World Order" which includes the New World Economy. One U.N. delegate actually proposed that corporations be asked to sponsor U.N. military forces the way they now do sports teams.

Notes to Chapter Four
The Flawed Debate

1. See Herman E. Daly and John B. Cobb, Jr., *For the Common Good: Redirecting the Economy Toward Community*, second edition (Boston: Beacon Press, 1994) for a further critique of the confounding of free trade and capital mobility.

2. Walter Wriston, "The Decline of the Central Bankers," op ed, *The New York Times*, September 20, 1992.

3. Strengthening national competitiveness should not be confused with strengthening national autonomy and self-reliance. For advocacy of the latter, see, for example, Daly and Cobb, *For the Common Good*, Samir Amin, *Delinking: Toward a Polycentric World* (London: Zed, 1990), and Tim Lang and Colon Hines, *The New Protectionism: Protecting the Future Against Free Trade* (New York: The New Press, 1993). These approaches, while in some sense "nationalist," are radically different from those discussed in this section. Most such "decentralists" turn out on close reading to advocate multilevel systems involving some degree of supra-national regulation. A comparison of various decentralist approaches, along with "global Keynesian" and other approaches that stress supranational regulation, would be a useful project, but one which lies beyond the scope of this book.

4. Michael Specter, "Great Russia Will Live Again," *The New York Times Magazine*, June 19, 1994, p. 56.

5. In Canada, the anti-NAFTA coalition was originally named the Pro-Canada Network, but changed its name to the Action Canada Network to soften the nationalist flavor.

6. Emir Sader and Ken Silverstein, *Without Fear of Being Happy* (London: Verso, 1991), p. 162.

7. This represents the beginning of a complex historical effort to disentangle the impulse to democratic self-rule from the legal doctrine of state sovereignty and the nationalist deification of the nation. To the extent

that nations represent historically established communities, and to the extent that national states represent the will of those they govern, they are no doubt appropriate vehicles for self-goverment. But there is no reason they should be the exclusive vehicles for self-government. Self-government is needed at every level from local to global. In some ways this approach resembles that of 18th century, pre-nationalist republican theory, which regarded representative forms of government as essential everywhere but did not particularly connect them with the nation state.

The controversy between national sovereignty and transnationally defined human rights goes back at least to the international movement to abolish slavery. The British blockade against the Atlantic slave trade was attacked as a violation of Spanish sovereignty and (with considerable justification) as an expression of British imperialism.

8. "Some Thoughts on the GATT Campaign," John Cavanagh, memo of January 13, 1994.

9. Richard Falk, "The Making of Global Citizenship" in Jeremy Brecher, John Brown Childs, and Jill Cutler, eds., *Global Visions: Beyond the New World Order* (Boston: South End Press, 1993), pp. 39-40.

Notes to Chapter Five
Resistance Is Global

1. *The American Political Report,* December 17, 1993. Kevin Philips was chief political analyst for the 1968 Republican presidential campaign and the architect of Richard Nixon's "Southern strategy."

2. *The New York Times,* December 17, 1990.

3. *Bankcheck Quarterly,* July 1992, p. 10.

4. *The New York Times,* May 9, 1994.

5. *The American Political Report,* December 17, 1993. Sebastian Edwards, the World Bank's chief economist for Latin America and the Caribbean, described the election as part of a consistent message that "economic reforms have not been consolidated in Latin America." Daniel Hellinger, "Venezuelan Electorate Applies Political Shock to Bankers," *Bankcheck Quarterly,* January, 1994.

6. Gay Seidman, "Facing the New International Context of Development," in Jeremy Brecher, John Brown Childs, and Jill Cutler, eds., *Global Visions: Beyond the New World Order* (Boston: South End Press, 1993), p. 178.

7. Peter Dorman, "Trade, Competition, and Jobs: An Internationalist Strategy," unpublished paper, September 1990, p. 8.

8. Seidman, in *Global Visions,* p. 177.

9. *LRA's Economic Notes,* October 1993, p. 7.

10. Seidman, p. 178.

11. Seidman, p. 178.

12. *The Economist*, December 11, 1993, cited in *The American Political Report*, December 17, 1993.

13. *Washington Times*, December 13, 1994, quoted in *The American Political Report*, December 17, 1993; *The New York Times*, May 31, 1994.

14. "Poles Hold March Over New Budget," *The New York Times*, February 10, 1994. It is often forgotten that the Polish Solidarity union originally formed in response to an austerity drive by Communist Poland that resulted from demands of western banks for loan repayment.

15. Don Fitz, "General Strike in Spain Fights Labor Law 'Reform'," *Labor Notes*, March 1994.

16. David Peterson, "The New Solidarity," Z, February 1994, p. 9. The Belgian cutback proposals were driven by fear of currency speculation and capital flight; without the cutbacks, according to the *Financial Times*, "officials and economists expect renewed pressures on the Belgian franc."

17. *The American Political Report*, December 17, 1993.

18. *The New York Times*, April 28, 1994.

19. Elaine Bernard, "The New Democratic Party and Labor Political Action in Canada," *Labor Research Review*, Summer 1994.

20. The politics of this shift is a central focus of Bob Woodward's book *The Agenda: Inside the Clinton White House* (New York: Simon and Schuster, 1994).

21. *The New York Times*, May 31, 1994.

22. Bruce Rich, *Mortgaging the Earth* (Boston: Beacon Press, 1994), p. 81. Figure corrected for inflation.

23. Rich, pp. 113-127.

24. Rich, pp. 128-131.

25. Rich, pp. 132-134.

26. Rich, p. 138.

27. *Bankcheck Quarterly*, January 1994; September 1993.

28. *The Washington Post*, June 19, 1994.

29. *Bankcheck Quarterly*, November 1992.

30. *Bankcheck Quarterly*, September 1993.

31. Pharis Harvey, "Development Banks to be Monitored for Labor Rights Violations," *Worker Rights News*, Summer 1994, p. 2.

32. Ritchie notes that contacts from the Nestlé boycott and the Highlander Center's 50th anniversary also helped provide links for the network.

33. Interview with Mark Ritchie.

34. Bernard quips that when George Bush said he wanted "a kinder and gentler country," many Canadians feared he was threatening to annex Canada.

35. Dan Goldrich, "Report to Activists of the Citizens Trade Campaign: Reflections on the Struggle Over NAFTA and Beyond," unpublished paper, May 1994.

36. Goldrich, p. 23. Goldrich notes that "It seems to me possible that the asser- tive solidarity stances noted above preempted and possibly transformed much of whatever potential for racism existed within the ranks of the coali- tions, and possibly even outside them. In other words, the definition of the situation as calling for solidarity may have created a political environment that dampened the tendency toward expressing racism."

37. Mary McGinn, quoted in Howard H. Frederick, "North American NGO Computer Networking Against NAFTA: The Use of Computer Commu- nications in Cross-Border Coalition-Building," paper presented at the XVII International Congress of the Latin American Studies Association, September 24-27, 1994, Los Angeles, California.

38. Alliance for Responsible Trade, Citizens Trade Campaign, Mexican Action Network on Free Trade, and Action Canada Network, *A Just and Sustainable Trade and Development Initiative for North America*, 1994.

Notes to Chapter Six
The Lilliput Strategy

1. Sierra Club, February, 1994.

2. Statement of UAW Secretary-Treasurer Bill Casstevens, quoted in *Peo- ple's Tribune* (Online Edition), vol. 21 no. 18, May 2, 1994.

3. Ibid.

4. Jorge G. Castañeda, *Utopia Unarmed* (New York: Knopf, 1993), 443ff.

5. Castañeda notes that such change depends on "significant modifications in the mainstream American outlook on economic and social matters."

6. A similar trade-off was made in the EC. c.f. Ian Robinson, *North Ameri- can Trade as if Democracy Mattered: What's Wrong with NAFTA and What Are the Alternatives?* (Ottawa and Washington, D.C.: Canadian Centre for Policy Alternatives and International Labor Rights Education and Research Fund, 1993).

7. Interview with Ron Blackwell, Amalgamated Clothing and Textile Workers Union.

8. "Toward a New North-South Economic Dialogue," in *Third World Re- surgence*, August 1993, pp. 18-21.

9. Martin Hart-Landsberg, "Post-NAFTA Politics: Learning from Asia," *Monthly Review*, June 1994. For additional reporting on PP21, see *AMPO: Ja- pan-Asia Quarterly Review*. "For an Alliance of Hope," Muto Ichiyo's key- note address for the first PP21 gathering, is published in Jeremy Brecher, John Brown Childs, and Jill Cutler, eds., *Global Visions: Beyond the New World Order*, (Boston: South End Press, 1993).

10. For additional analysis of such convergence processes, see Jeremy Bre- cher and Tim Costello, *Building Bridges: The Emerging Grassroots Coalition of Labor and Community* (New York: Monthly Review Press, 1990).

11. The contribution of World Bank staff to this process is indicated by the impressive number of leaked documents which find their way into the pages of *Bankcheck Quarterly*.

12. See Jane Slaughter, "Corporate Campaigns: Labor Enlists Community Support" in Brecher and Costello, *Building Bridges*.

Notes to Chapter Seven
Global Rules

1. Steve Charnovitz, "International Trade and Worker Rights," *SAIS Review*, Winter-Spring 1987, vol. 7, no. 1, p. 189. The National Recovery Act even empowered the President to restrict imports that would undermine the codes.

2. Of course, raising decisionmaking to a higher federal level can also be used by business to outflank popular movements; a classic case was the federalization of commerce and anti-trust policy in the late 19th century as a vehicle to head off agrarian radicalism and its "granger" laws. This parallels current efforts to "pre-empt" local and national legislation via GATT.

3. See Lochner *v.* New York, 1905.

4. Paul C. Stern, Oran R. Young, and Daniel Druckman, eds., *Global Environmental Change: Understanding the Human Dimension* (Washington, D.C.: National Academy Press, 1992).

5. Charnovitz, *SAIS Review*, p. 192. In the late 1980s, German and South African metal unions drew up a 14-point code of labor rights which the German unions pressured Daimler-Benz, Volkswagen, and other leading German companies to sign. Denis MacShane, "Human Rights and Labour Rights," March 1992 (unpublished paper).

6. "The Denim Revolution: Levi Strauss & Co. Adopts a Code of Conduct," February 1994 research report, Council on Economic Priorities. All information on corporate sourcing guidelines is from this report, unless otherwise noted.

    The Levi Strauss code has by no means eliminated all abuses. One investigator, for example, interviewed more than a dozen women who had worked at Intersew, a recently closed Levi Strauss contractor in Juarez, Mexico, who told her that children under 14 worked in the plant and that the roof leaked so badly that workers got electric shocks from their sewing machines. A Levi Strauss spokesperson denied the allegations and stated an audit of the plant found it "in compliance with our sourcing guidelines." Laurie Udesky, "Sweatshops Behind the Labels," *The Nation*, May 16, 1994.

7. CBS, July 2, 1993, cited in "The Denim Revolution."

8. Interview with Ron Blackwell, January 13, 1994.

9. *Fact Finding Report*, Washington, D.C.: Commission on the Future of Worker-Management Relations (Dunlap Commission), May 1994, p. 70.

Other common U.S. practices which violate internationally recognized labor rights and standards include child labor, sweatshop conditions, wage discrimination, sexual harassment, sub-poverty minimum wage, excessive hours of labor, lack of job security, and lack of protection against arbitrary discharge.

10. See Jeremy Brecher, "May Day," *Strike!* (Boston: South End Press, 1977).

11. Charnovitz, *SAIS Review*, p. 188.

12. Charnovitz, pp. 188-189; *The International Labor Organization: Backgrounder* (Washington, D.C.: ILO Bureau of Public Information, December 1993).

13. *The International Labor Organization: Backgrounder.*

14. *The International Labor Organization: Backgrounder*; Charnovitz.

15. Economist Peter Dorman, who has written extensively on labor rights, points out that such rights, like other rights, "are simply those which workers have been able to win in particular contexts, generalized to everyone." They do not necessarily imply western theories of social contract or natural law; rather, they are values and policies expressed in a language which makes them potentially enforceable. For a discussion of the historical character of rights, and of labor rights in particular, see Staughton Lynd, "Communal Rights," *Texas Law Review,* May 1984.

16. Renfrey Clarke, "E-mail Helps Win Release of Political Prisoners," *Net-News,* January/February 1994.

17. Charnovitz, *SAIS Review,* p. 185.

18. Charnovitz, p. 189.

19. Charnovitz, p. 190.

20. The term "social dumping" has been used widely in European discussions to refer to trade practices in which product prices are unfairly lowered through illegitimate labor practices.

21. Ray Marshall, "Workers Need International Code to Protect Their Rights," *Los Angeles Times,* July 26, 1987.

22. *Worker Rights News,* Winter 1994.

23. *Worker Rights News,* Winter 1994.

24. *The New York Times,* editorial, January 15, 1994.

25. *Wall Street Journal,* February 10, 1994, cited in *Worker Rights News,* Winter 1994.

26. Unpublished report on informal consultations held in September 1987, on formation of a labor rights working party in GATT.

27. See John Cavanagh, "Strategies to Advance Labor and Environmental Standards: A North-South Dialogue," *Capitalism, Nature, Socialism,* September 1993.

28. Interview on National Public Radio's *All Things Considered,* April 15, 1994.

29. Pratap Chatterjee, "World Trade: Workers' rights plan splits governments and activists" an Inter Press Service feature, April 8, 1994.

30. "Why GATT and the WTO Should Not Deal with Labour Standards" and "Why the WTO Should Not Deal with Labour Standards," *Third World Network Features*, April 8, 1994 and April 21, 1994.

31. Chatterjee, "World Trade." Takashi Izumi, general secretary of the International Confederation of Free Trade Unions, Asian and Pacific Regional Organization argues "What needs to be agreed upon globally is that discrimination, forced labor, especially by children, and restrictions on workers' ability to form free trade unions to bargain with employers are unacceptable in an increasingly global market. Developing countries in Asia that are trying to improve the conditions of workers are in fact the most vulnerable to effects of such practices on the competitiveness of their products and services." "A Chance for Labor in Asia," *International Herald Tribune*, April 4, 1994.

32. This discussion draws on the work of John Cavanagh, including "Strategies to Advance Labor and Environmental Standards: A North-South Dialogue," *Capitalism, Nature, Socialism*, September 1993; several unpublished memos; and several interviews. Other suggestions come from discussions with Primitivo Rodriguez, Peter Dorman, and Pharis Harvey.

33. Peter Dorman has suggested as a first step an international labor court of appeals along the lines of the European Court of Justice and the World Court. It would have jurisdiction over appeals of labor rights cases involving national labor rights statutes and a core of basic international labor rights. It would be less sweeping than GATT conditionality because it would focus on cases rather than national policies. It would apply to industrialized as well as poor countries—for example, it could consider non-enforcement of the U.S. National Labor Relations Act.

34. See Chapter Six for further discussion of the "Grand Bargain."

35. Ian Robinson, *North American Trade as if Democracy Mattered: What's Wrong with NAFTA and What Are the Alternatives?* (Ottawa and Washington, D.C.: Canadian Centre for Policy Alternatives and International Labor Rights Education and Research Fund, 1993), p. 29.

36. Longtime British labor activist Ken Coates has proposed citizen action to counter the British opt out. "Customers are not obliged to purchase goods which are produced under adverse conditions, and offer unfair competition. Even if the British government maintains its refusal to apply minimum European standards, there will be strong pressure on individual companies to accept them. One way of increasing this pressure would be to institute a European social compliance badge, which could be affixed...to all goods which were manufactured in conformity with European rules....Employers and exporters would be likely to conform to European standards rather quickly, if the penalty for non-compliance was loss of market share." *Chartist*, July-August 1993.

37. Many efforts in this direction are under way. For example, besides efforts to establish a labor rights working party in GATT, there are efforts to incorporate labor rights in the Asia Pacific Economic Cooperation,

MERCOSUR, and the agreements to extend NAFTA to additional countries. Revelations that the U.S. Agency for International Development (AID) was encouraging U.S. companies to relocate in Central America to take advantage of cheap labor and the repression of unions led Congress in 1993 to prohibit "assistance for any project or activity that contributes to the violation of internationally recognized worker rights"—a provision arguably applicable to multilateral financial institutions like the World Bank.

Notes to Chapter Eight
Labor in the New World Economy

1. *Beehive*, December 5, 1863, quoted in Peter Waterman, "The Dramatic Rise and Strange Decline of Proletarian Internationalism," in *The Old Internationalism and the New*, Peter Waterman, ed. (The Hague: International Labour Education, Research and Information Foundation, 1988), pp. 22-23. See this and other work by Peter Waterman for analysis of labor internationalism in general.

2. Denis MacShane, *International Labour and the Origins of the Cold War*, (Oxford: Clarendon Press, 1992), p. 10.

3. Samuel Gompers, *Seventy Years of Life and Labor*, (New York: E.P. Dutton, 1957), p. 280.

4. See Steven Fraser, *Labor Will Rule: Sidney Hillman and the Rise of American Labor*, (New York: The Free Press, 1991).

5. Fraser, pp. 542-543.

6. Fraser, p. 547.

7. MacShane, p. 280.

8. *Business Week*, May 15, 1966, quoted in Beth Sims, *Workers of the World Undermined: American Labor's Role in U.S. Foreign Policy* (Boston: South End Press, 1992).

9. William Serrin, "Labor as Usual," *Village Voice*, February 23, 1988. Also see Sims, *Workers of the World Undermined*, for more on the role of the AFL-CIO's international affairs operation.

10. *Labor Notes*, February 1994, p. 14.

11. *Labor Notes*, February 1994, p. 14.

12. "Which Side (Of the Border) Are You On? Well, Both." *Business Week*, April 4, 1994, p. 50.

13. "How the USW Hit Marc Rich Where It Hurts," *Business Week*, May 11, 1992, p. 42.

14. *LRA's Economic Notes*, May-June 1992, pp. 3-6.

15. *Business Week*, May 11, 1992.

16. "World Unions Take on Caterpillar," *AFL-CIO News*, February 7, 1994.

17. *Worker Rights News*, Summer 1994.

18. "IAM Forges Air Alliances," *AFL-CIO News*, April 18, 1994.

19. Peter Waterman, "International Labour Communication by Computer: The Fifth International?" Working Paper Series No. 129 (The Hague: Institute of Social Studies, 1992).

20. Richard B. Freeman and Joel Rogers, "Who Speaks for Us? Employee Representation in a Non-Union Labor Market" in Industrial Relations Research Association, ed., *Employee Representation: Alternatives and Future Directions* (Madison: Industrial Relations Research Association, 1993), p. 13.

21. *LRA's Economic Notes*, April 1993, p. 7.

22. Gary N. Chaison and Dileep G. Dhavale, "A Note on the Severity of the Decline in Union Organizing Activity," *Industrial and Labor Relations Review*, vol. 43, 1990, in Freeman and Rogers.

23. "The ICFTU in South Africa," *South African Labour Bulletin*, vol. 17, no. 1, January-February, 1993.

24. "The new world economy—challenge by labor" in *South African Labour Bulletin*, September/October, 1993.

25. "ICFTU: Boost World Output, Close Social Gap," *Workers' Education*, June 1994. For further discussion of the "trade union strategy for world development," see Chapter Nine.

26. Peter Waterman, "The ICFTU in SA: Admissions, Revelations, Silences," *South African Labour Bulletin*, vol. 17, no. 3, May/June, 1993.

Notes to Chapter Nine
Reversing the Race to the Bottom

1. Such common interests do not eliminate all conflict. Some may be threatened more than others; some may benefit from activities or policies which cause environmental damage; environmental protection may be more costly for some than for others. These factors modify, but do not refute, the existence of a common human interest in the global environment.

2. See footnote 10 in Introduction for examples.

3. Roughly equivalent to what this book has referred to as the Corporate Agenda.

4. See Vandana Shiva, "The Greening of the Global Reach," in Jeremy Brecher, John Brown Childs, and Jill Cutler, eds., *Global Visions: Beyond the New World Order* (Boston: South End Press, 1993). Mark Ritchie notes that the United Nations Economic and Social Council (ECOSOC) was given broad powers by Chapter X of the U.N. Charter to coordinate the policies and activities of the specialized agencies, which include the World Bank, IMF, and GATT. Ritchie argues that this provides a potential framework for the democratization of those institutions. Mark Ritchie, "Back to the Future: Energize ECOSOC," *Why.*, Summer 1994, p. 11.

5. For further discussion of the necessity for global demand management see Robert Kuttner, *The End of Laissez-Faire* (New York: Knopf, 1991).

6. Walter Russell Mead, "The United States and the World Economy: Part II," *World Policy Journal*, vol. VI, no. 3, summer 1989. For a somewhat less ambitious proposal along similar lines, see Howard M. Wachtel's *The Money Mandarins: The Making of a Supranational Economic Order* (Armonk, NY: M.E. Sharp, 1990).

7. United Nations Development Program, *Human Development Report 1992* (New York: Oxford, 1992), pp. 78-9.

8. "ICFTU: Boost World Output, Close Social Gap," *Workers' Education*, June 1994, p. 10. The "trade union strategy for world development," developed jointly by the International Confederation of Free Trade Unions and the International Trade Secretariats, would use special drawing rights (SDRs) as the vehicle for expanding currency reserves.

9. See Chapter Seven above for more on the EU's "Social Dimension."

10. Alliance for Responsible Trade, Citizens Trade Campaign, Mexican Action Network on Free Trade, and Action Canada Network, *A Just and Sustainable Trade and Development Initiative for North America*, 1994.

11. The details of such a plan are spelled out in Susan George, *A Fate Worse than Debt: The World Financial Crisis and the Poor* (New York: Grove, Weidenfeld, 1990).

12. Third World Network, "Toward a New North-South Economic Dialogue," in *Third World Resurgence*, August 1993, pp. 18-21.

13. See Michael Barratt Brown, *Fair Trade: Reform and Realities in the International Trading System* (London: Zed, 1993).

14. Jeremy Brecher, *"Canst Thou Draw Out Leviathan with a Fishhook?" A Community-Based Response to an Out-of-Control Economy* (Washington: Grassroots Policy Project, in press).

15. Nancy Benson, "African Women Cooperate to Create Development Alternatives," *Listen Real Loud*, Vol. 12, No. 1.

16. Charles McCollester and Mike Stout, "Tri-State Conference on Steel: Ten years of a Labor-Community Alliance," in Jeremy Brecher and Tim Costello, eds., *Building Bridges: The Emerging Grassroots Coalition of Labor and Community* (New York: Monthly Review Press, 1990).

17. Jeremy Brecher, "How to Grow the Economy," op ed, *The Hartford Courant*, July 18, 1993.

18. Maureen Mackintosh and Hilary Wainwright, eds., *A Taste of Power: The Politics of Local Economics* (London: Verso, 1987).

19. Jeremy Brecher and Paul Kumar, "Putting Connecticut Back to Work," *The New Haven Advocate*, January 21, 1993.

20. See Jeremy Brecher and Tim Costello, eds., *Building Bridges: The Emerging Grassroots Coalition of Labor and Community* (New York: Monthly Review Press, 1990).

21. Even conventional economists increasingly emphasize the measurably high returns to education and healthcare and the negative effects of inadequate investment in public infrastructure. The "economic miracle" NICs of eastern Asia are notable for their high level of investment in education.

22. "Total military expenditures worldwide in 1991 were $1,038 trillion... The United States is still spending nearly as much as the rest of the world combined." Editorial, *The New York Times*, May 30, 1994.

Resources

Books

Amin, Samir. *Delinking: Towards a Polycentric World*. London: Zed, 1990.

Amott, Theresa, *Caught in the Crisis: Women and the U.S. Economy Today*. New York: Monthly Review Press, 1993.

Barnet, Richard J. and John Cavanagh. *Global Dreams: Imperial Corporations and the New World Order*. New York: Simon and Schuster, 1994.

Bartlett, Donald L. and James B. Steele. *America: What Went Wrong?* Kansas City: Andrews & McMeel, 1992.

Bello, Walden. *Dragons in Distress: Asia's Miracle Economics in Crisis*. London: Penguin, 1991.

Bello, Walden, with Shea Cunningham and Bill Rau. *Dark Victory: The United States, Structural Adjustment and Global Poverty*. Oakland, California: Food First, 1994.

Bluestone, Barry and Bennett Harrison. *The Deindustrialization of America: Plant Closings, Community Abandonment, and the Dismantling of Basic Industry*. New York: Basic Books, 1982.

Bluestone, Barry and Bennett Harrison. *The Great U-Turn: Corporate Restructuring and the Polarization of America*. New York: Basic Books, 1988.

Brecher, Jeremy. *Strike!* Boston: South End Press, 1977.

Brecher, Jeremy and Tim Costello, eds. *Building Bridges: The Emerging Grassroots Coalition of Labor and Community.* New York: Monthly Review Press, 1990.

Brecher, Jeremy and Tim Costello. *Global Village vs. Global Pillage: A One-World Strategy for Labor.* Washington, D.C.: International Labor Rights Education and Research Fund, 1991.

Brecher, Jeremy, John Brown Childs, and Jill Cutler, eds. *Global Visions: Beyond the New World Order.* Boston: South End Press, 1993.

Broad, Robin, with John Cavanagh. *Plundering Paradise: The Struggle for the Environment in the Philippines.* Berkeley and Los Angeles: University of California Press, 1993.

Brown, Michael Barratt. *Fair Trade: Reform and Realities in the International Trading System.* London: Zed, 1993.

Browne, Harry and Beth Sims. *Runaway America: U.S. Jobs and Factories on the Move.* Albuquerque, New Mexico: Resource Center Press, 1993.

Cantor, Daniel and Juliet Schor. *Tunnel Vision: Labor, the World Economy, and Central America.* Boston: South End Press, 1987.

Castañeda, Jorge G. *Utopia Unarmed: The Latin American Left after the Cold War.* New York: Knopf, 1993.

Cavanagh, John, John Gershman, Karen Baker, and Gretchen Helmke, eds. *Trading Freedom: How Free Trade Affects Our Lives, Work, and Environment.* San Francisco: Food First, 1992.

Chomsky, Noam. *Year 501: The Conquest Continues.* Boston: South End Press, 1993.

Daly, Herman E. and John B. Cobb, Jr. *For the Common Good: Redirecting the Economy Toward Community, the Environment, and a Sustainable Future,* second edition. Boston: Beacon Press, 1994.

Danaher, Kevin, ed., *50 Years Is Enough: The Case Against The World Bank and the International Monetary Fund.* Boston: South End Press, 1994.

Earth Island Press, ed. *The Case Against Free Trade: GATT, NAFTA, and the Globalization of Corporate Power.* San Francisco: Earth Island Press, 1993.

Epstein, Gerald, Julie Graham, and Jessica Nembhard. *Creating a New World Economy: Forces of Change and Plans for Action.* Philadelphia: Temple University Press, 1993.

Falk, Richard. *Explorations at the Edge of Time.* Philadelphia: Temple University Press, 1992.

Ferguson, Thomas and Joel Rogers. *The Hidden Election: Politics and Economics in the 1980 Presidential Campaign.* New York: Pantheon Books, 1981.

Fraser, Steven. *Labor Will Rule: Sidney Hillman and the Rise of American Labor.* New York: The Free Press, 1991.

Fraser, Steve and Gary Gerstle, eds. *The Rise and Fall of the New Deal Order, 1930-1980.* Princeton: Princeton University Press, 1989.

George, Susan. *The Debt Boomerang: How Third World Debt Harms Us All.* London: Pluto Press, 1992.

George, Susan. *A Fate Worse Than Debt: The World Financial Crisis and the Poor.* New York: Grove, Weidenfeld, 1990.

Harrison, Bennett. *Lean and Mean: The Changing Landscape of Corporate Power in the Age of Flexibility.* New York: Basic Books, 1994.

Harvey, David. *The Condition of Postmodernity.* Oxford: Basil Blackwell, 1989.

Hecker, Steven and Margaret Hallock, eds. *Labor in a Global Economy: Perspectives from the U.S. and Canada.* Eugene, Oregon: University of Oregon Books, 1991.

Herzenberg, Stephen and Jorge Perez-Lopez, eds. *Labor Standards and Development in the Global Economy.* Washington, D.C.: U.S. Department of Labor, 1990.

Jenson, Jane and Rianne Mahan, eds. *The Challenge of Restructuring: North American Labor Movements Respond.* Philadelphia: Temple University Press, 1993.

Kamel, Rachael. *The Global Factory: Analysis and Action for a New Economic Era.* Philadelphia: American Friends Service Committee, 1990.

Kennedy, Paul. *Preparing for the Twenty-First Century.* New York: Random House, 1993.

Khor Kok Peng, Martin. *The Future of North-South Relations: Conflict or Cooperation?* Penang: Third World Network, 1992.

Kolko, Joyce. *Restructuring the World Economy.* New York: Pantheon, 1988.

Korten,. David C. *Getting to the 21st Century: Voluntary Action and the Global Agenda.* West Hartford, CT: Kumarian Press, 1990.

Kutner, Robert. *The End of Laissez-Faire.* New York: Knopf, 1991.

MacShane, Denis. *International Labour and the Origins of the Cold War.* Oxford: Clarendon Press, 1992.

La Botz, Dan. *Mask of Democracy: Labor Suppression in Mexico Today.* Boston: SouthEnd Press, 1992.

Lang, Tim and Colon Hines. *The New Protectionism: Protecting the Future Against Free Trade.* New York: The New Press, 1993.

Lipietz, Alain. *Towards a New Economic Order.* New York: Oxford University Press, 1992.

MacEwan, Arthur and William K. Tabb, *Instability and Change in the World Economy*. New York: Monthly Review Press, 1989.

Mann, Michael. *The Sources of Social Power: Volume I: A history of power from the beginning to A.D. 1760*. Cambridge: Cambridge University Press, 1986.

Mann, Michael. *The Sources of Social Power: Volume II: The rise of classes and nation-states, 1760-1940*. Cambridge: Cambridge University Press, 1993.

Margolin, Stephen and Juliet Schor. *The End of the Golden Age*. New York: Oxford University Press, 1989.

Marshall, Ray. *Unheard Voices: Labor and Economic Policy in a Competitive World*. New York: Basic Books, 1987.

Mead, Walter Russell. *The Low-Wage Challenge to Global Growth: The Labor Cost-Productivity Imbalance in Newly Industrializing Countries*. Washington: Economic Policy Institute, 1991.

Mishel, Lawrence and Jared Bernstein, *The State of Working America: 1992-93*. Washington: Economic Policy Institute, 1993.

Moody, Kim and Mary McGinn. *Unions and Free Trade: Solidarity vs. Competition*. Detroit: Labor Notes, 1992.

Peceira, Luiz Carlos Bressor, Jose Maria Maravall, and Adam Przeworski. *Economic Reforms in New Democracies: A Social-Democratic Approach*. Cambridge: Cambridge University Press, 1993.

Philips, Kevin. *The Politics of Rich and Poor*. New York: HarperPerennial, 1991.

Philips, Kevin. *Boiling Point: Democrats, Republicans, and the Decline of Middle-Class Prosperity*. New York: Random House, 1993.

Przeworski, Adam. *Democracy and the Market: Political and Economic Reforms in Eastern Europe and Latin America*. Cambridge: Cambridge University Press, 1992.

Raghavan, Chakravarthi. *Recolonization: GATT, the Uruguay Round, and the Third World*. Penang, Malaysia: Third World Network, 1990.

Ranney, David C. *The Evolving Supra-National Policy Arena*. Chicago: University of Illinois at Chicago, Center for Urban Economic Development, 1993.

Reich, Robert B. *The Work of Nations: Preparing Ourselves for 21st Century Capitalism*. New York: Vintage, 1992.

Rich, Bruce. *Mortgaging the Earth: The World Bank, Environmental Impoverishment and the Crisis of Development*. Boston: Beacon Press, 1994.

Robinson, Ian. *North American Trade as if Democracy Mattered: What's Wrong with NAFTA and What Are the Alternatives?*. Ottawa and

Washington: Canadian Centre for Policy Alternatives and International Labor Rights Education and Research Fund, 1993.

Rowbotham, Sheila and Swasti Mitter, eds. *Dignity and Daily Bread: New forms of economic organizing among poor women in the Third World and the First.* London and New York: Routledge, 1994.

Sassen, Saskia. *Globalization and its Discontents.* New York: New Press, 1998.

Schor, Juliet. *The Overworked American.* New York: Basic Books, 1991.

Sims, Beth. *Workers of the World Undermined: American Labor's Role in U.S. Foreign Policy.* Boston: South End Press, 1992.

Skinner, Quentin. *The Foundations of Modern Political Thought.* Cambridge: Cambridge University Press, 1987.

Sklar, Holly. *The Trilateral Commission and Elite Planning for World Management.* Boston: South End Press, 1980.

United Nations Development Programme. *Human Development Report 1992.* New York: Oxford University Press, 1992.

United Nations Development Programme. *Human Development Report 1993.* New York: Oxford University Press, 1993.

United States Congress, Office of Technology Assessment. *U.S.-Mexico Free Trade: Pulling Together or Pulling Apart?* Washington: Government Printing Office, October 1992.

Wachtel, Howard. *The Money Mandarins: The Making of a New Supranational Economic Order.* New York: Pantheon, 1986.

Ward, Kathryn, ed. *Women Workers and Global Restructuring.* Ithaca, NY: ILR Press, 1990.

Waterman, Peter. *The Old Internationalism and the New.* The Hague: International Labour Education, Research and Information Foundation, 1988.

Wriston, Walter. *The Twilight of Sovereignty.* New York: Macmillan, 1992.

Yates, Michael D. *Longer Hours, Fewer Jobs: Employment & Unemployment in the United States.* New York: Monthly Review Press, 1994.

Articles and Papers

Alliance for Responsible Trade, Citizens Trade Campaign, Mexican Action Network on Free Trade, and Action Canada Network. "A Just and Sustainable Trade and Development Initiative for North America." 1994.

American Friends Service Committee. "From Global Pillage to Global Village: A Perspective from Working People and People of Color on the Unregulated Internationalization of the Economy." (Statement endorsed by sixty grassroots organizations.) Philadelphia: American Friends Service Committee, 1994.

Brecher, Jeremy. "The 'National Question' Reconsidered," *New Politics*, Summer, 1987.

Brecher, Jeremy. "Crisis Economy: Born-Again Labor Movement?" *Monthly Review*, March, 1984.

Charnovitz, Steve. "International Trade and Worker Rights," *SAIS Review*, Winter-Spring 1987, Volume 7, No. 1.

Coalition for Justice in the Maquiladoras. "Maquiladora Standards of Conduct." San Antonio, Texas: Coalition for Justice in the Maquiladoras, 1992.

Dorman, Peter. "Worker Rights and U.S. Trade Policy: An Evaluation of Worker Rights Conditionality Under the General System of Preferences." Washington: Bureau of International Labor Affairs, U.S. Department of Labor, September, 1989.

Freeman, Richard B. and Joel Rogers. "Who Speaks for Us? Employee Representation in a Non-Union Labor Market," in *Employee Representation: Alternatives and Future Directions*. Madison: Industrial Relations Research Association, 1993.

Gallon, Dan. "Drawing the Battle Lines," *New Politics*, Summer, 1994.

Herzenberg, Stephen. "Institutionalizing Constructive Competition: International Labor Standards and Trade." Economic Discussion Paper No. 32. Washington: Bureau of International Affairs, U.S. Department of Labor, September, 1988.

International Metalworkers Federation. "IMF Action Programme, 1993-1997." Geneva: International Metalworkers Federation, 1993.

Levinson, Jerome I. "Failed Mission: Financing Latin American Development." Twentieth Century Fund.

Mead, Walter Russell. "The United States and the World Economy: Part II." *World Policy Journal*, Volume VI, No. 3, Summer 1989.

Ranney, David C. and William Cecil. "Transnational Investment and Job Loss in Chicago: Impacts on Women, African-Americans and Latinos." Chicago: University of Illinois at Chicago, Center for Urban Economic Development, January, 1993.

Rothstein, Richard. "Setting the Standard: International Labor Rights and U.S. Trade Policy." Washington, D.C.: Economic Policy Institute, March 1993.

Ruggie, John Gerard. "Territoriality and Beyond" *International Organization*, Vol. 47, Winter, 1993.

Periodicals

The American Political Report. 7316 Wisconsin Avenue, Bethesda, Maryland 20814. $125/year.

AMPO: Japan-Asia Quarterly Review. Pacific Asia Resource Center, PO Box 5250, Tokyo International, Japan. $24/year.

Bankcheck Quarterly. 1847 Berkeley Way, Berkeley, CA 94703. $25/year.

Beyond Borders: A forum for labor in action around the globe. 4677 30th Street, Suite 214, San Diego, CA 02116. $16/year.

Dollars and Sense. 1 Summer Street, Somerville, MA 02143. $22.95/year.

Grassroots Economic Organizing Newsletter. PO Box 5065, New Haven, CT 06525. $15/year.

Labor Notes, 7435 Michigan Ave., Detroit, MI 48210. $20/year.

Labor Research Review. Midwest Center for Labor Research, 3411 West Diversey Avenue, Suite 10, Chicago, IL 60647. $15/year.

LRA's Economic Notes: News and Analysis for Trade Unionists. 145 West 28th Street, 6th floor, New York, NY 10001. $30/year.

Left Business Observer. 250 West 85th St., New York, NY 10024. $20/year.

Peace and Democracy. P.O. Box 1640, Cathedral Station, New York, NY 10025. $7/year.

South African Labour Bulletin, P.O. Box 3851, Johannesburg, 2000, South Africa. $52/year.

Third World Resurgence, c/o Michelle Syverson & Associates, P.O. Box 680, Manzanita, OR 97130. $20/year.

Worker Rights News. International Labor Rights Education and Research Fund, 100 Maryland Avenue, NE, Box 74, Washington, DC 20002. $15/year.

Working Together: Labor Report on the Americas, Resource Center of the Americas, 317 17th Ave., SE, Minneapolis, MN 55414.

Film and Video

All Work and No Play: NAFTA's Impact on Child Labor. Child Labor Coalition, c/o National Consumer's League, Washington, DC.

The Business of America. California Newsreel, 149 9th Street, #420 San Francisco, CA, 94193. 45 minutes.

Cross Border Organizing, A Response to NAFTA. Support Committee for Maquiladora Workers, PO Box 86479, San Diego, CA 92138. 10 minutes.

Dirty Business: Food Exports to the United States. Migrant Media Productions, Box 2048, Freedom, CA 95019. 15 minutes.

Four Dollars a Day?/No Way. American Labor Education Center, 2000 P St., NW, #300, Washington, DC 20036. 20 minutes.

Free Trade, Who's Gonna Pay? Labor Education Service of University of Minnesota, 437 Management and Economics Building, University of Minnesota, Minneapolis, MN 55455.

From the Mountains to the Maquiladoras. The Tennessee Industrial Renewal Network, 1515 E. Magnolia Ave, Suite 403, Knoxville, TN 37917. 615/637-1576. 25 minutes. $13 postpaid.

Global Assembly Line. New Day films, 853 Broadway, Rm. 1210, New York, NY 10003. 1 hour.

Interview with Santos Martinez. Windsor Occupational Safety and Health Group, 1731 Wyandotte St. E, Windsor, Ontario N8Y 1C9. 29 minutes. $25.

Mexico for Sale. Mexico Libre Productions, PO Box 20018, Altadena, CA 91001. $39.95 plus postage.

Roger and Me. Available at most video-rental stores. 106 minutes.

The Secret Side of Free Trade. Public Media Center. (202) 546-8630.

Stepan Chemical: The Poisoning of a Mexican Community. Coalition for Justice in the Maquiladoras, 3120 W. Ashby, San Antonio, TX 78228.

Trading Our Future. Institute for Agriculture and Trade Policy, 1313 Fifth St. SE, Suite 303, Minneapolis, MN 55414. 20 minutes. $30.

We Can Say No! 28 minutes. *Fighting Back.* 60 minutes. Action Canada Network, Suite 904, 251 Laurier West, Ottawa, Ontario, K1P 5J6. $34

Organizations

Action Canada Network, 904-251 Laurier Ave., West Ottawa, ON K1P 5J6 Canada.

American Friends Service Committee, Maqiladora Project, Women and Global Corporations Project, U.S.-Mexico Border Program, 1501 Cherry St., Philadelphia, PA 19102.

American Labor Education Center, 2000 P St. NW #300, Washington, DC 20036.

Bank Information Center, 2025 I St. NW, Suite 522, Washington, DC 20006.

Center of Concern, 3700 13th St. NE, Washington, DC 20017.

Citizens Trade Campaign, 600 Maryland Ave. SW, Washington, DC 20024.

Coalition for Justice in the Maquiladoras, 3120 West Ashby, San Antonio, TX 78228.

Development Group for Alternative Policies, 927 15th St. NW, 4th floor, Washington, DC 20005.

Economic Policy Institute, 1730 Rhode Island Ave. NW, Suite 200, Washington, DC 20036.

Greenpeace International, 1436 U St. NW, Washington, DC 20009.

Institute for Agriculture and Trade Policy, 1313 Fifth St. SE, Suite 303, Minneapolis, MN 55414-1546.

Institute for Food and Development Policy, 398 60th St. Oakland, CA 94618.

Institute for Global Communications, 18 De Boom St. San Francisco, CA 94107.

Institute for Policy Studies, 1601 Connecticut Ave. NW, Washington, DC 20009.

International Labor Rights Education and Research Fund, 100 Maryland Ave. NW, Box 74, Washington, DC 20002

International Labor Rights Education and Research Fund, 100 Maryland Ave. NW, Box 74, Washington, DC 20002.

Mujer a Mujer/Woman to Woman, 606 Shaw St., Toronto, Ontario M6G 3L6.

North American Worker-to-Worker Network, c/o *Labor Notes*, 7435 Michigan Ave., Detroit, MI 48210.

Red Mexicana de Accion Frente al Libre Comeracio/Mexican Action Network on Free Trade, No. 20 Calle Godard, Colonia Guardalupe Victoria, Mexico, D.F. 07790, Mexico.

Resource Center, Box 4506, Albuquerque, New Mexico 87196.

Third World Network, 228 Macalister Road, 10400, Penang, Malaysia.

Transnationals Information Exchange, 7435 Michigan Ave., Detroit, MI 48210.

Other Resources

For access to on-line networking, a good point of entry is the Institute for Global Communications with its PeaceNet, EcoNet, LaborNet, and other services. IGC electronic conferences consulted in the course of writing this book include act.wb, bitl.pen, econ.saps, greenleft.news, labr.cis, trade.library, trade.news, trade.strategy, intl.economics, carnet.mexnews, labr.global, labr.privatization, and women.labr. 18 De Boom Street, San Francisco, CA 94107. 415/442-0220. fax: 415/546-1794. e-mail: apcadmin@apc.org

WorldWise. *International Directory of Non-Governmental Organizations*. Sacramento, CA: WorldWise.

Index

Index

A

ACN. *See* Action Canada Network

Action Canada Network (ACN), 99-100

Activism. *See* Globalization resistance movement; Globalrules; Human Agenda; Labor internationalism; LilliputStrategy; Non-Governmental Organizations (NGOs)

ACTWU. *See* Amalgamated Clothing and Textile Workers Union

AFL. *See* American Federation of Labor

AFL-CIO. *See* American Federation of Labor-Congress ofIndustrial Organizations

Africa, 27-28, 30, 60, 114. *See also* Apartheid; SouthAfrica; *specific countries*

African National Congress, 114

Agency for International Development, 150

Agricultural Adjustment Act, 43

A Just and Sustainable Trade and Development Initiative forNorth America, 80, 101, 102, 110, 178-79

Amalgamated Clothing and Textile Workers Union (ACTWU), 127

Amazonian Alliance of the Peoples of the Forest, 92

Amazon rainforest, 91-92, 108, 114-15

American Federation of Labor (AFL), 146-47, 149

American Federation of Labor-Congress of Industrial Organizations (AFL-CIO), 133-34, 146-47, 148, 149, 150-51,153, 158, 161, 163

American Institute for Free Labor Development, 150

The American Political Report, 83, 89

Amnesty International, 127-28, 129

ANCOM. *See* Andean Common Market

Andean Common Market (ANCOM), 61

Antarctica Treaty, 122

Apartheid, 114, 123-24, 175

APEC. *See* Asian-Pacific Economic Council

ASEAN. *See* Association of Southeast Asian Nations

Asia, 24, 30-31, 52, 61, 92, 93, 135

Asian-Pacific Economic Council (APEC), 61

Asian-Pacific Peoples Environmental Network, 92

Asian People's Solidarity Against Debt and Recolonization, 93

Asian Tigers, 24, 52

Association of Southeast Asian Nations (ASEAN), 61, 135

Authentic Workers' Front (FAT), 156

Automobile industry, 16, 18, 21, 69, 115, 154-55, 156

B

Bacon, Kenneth H., 58

Bangkok Agreement, 61

Bangladesh, 93

Baumol, William, 21

Belgium, 7, 89, 158

Bernard, Elaine, 100

Berry, T. Scott, 17, 20

Blackwell, Ron, 127

BMW, 16, 21

Bolivia, 86

Boston Globe, 23
Brady Plan, 89-90
Brazil, 17, 87, 89-90, 135, 163; Amazon rainforest of, 91-92, 108, 114-15
Bretton Woods system, 30, 45-46, 49-50, 56
British Airways, 159
British Department of Trade and Industry, 16
Buchanan, Pat, 32
Bush, George, 61, 75, 99, 133
Business Week, 26, 52, 124, 150, 157, 158

C

CACM. *See* Central American Common Market
Canada: and globalization resistance movement, 8, 89, 90, 93, 155; and Montreal Protocol, 122-23; and North AmericanFree Trade Agreement (NAFTA), 6, 61, 75-76, 79-80, 97-102, 197n5; and Ontario Federation of Labour, 90; andunemployment, 27
Capitalism, 17, 37-38, 89, 194n4; and democracy, 39-40; anddownward spiral, 42-43, 50; and industrialism, 40, 145-47; and markets, 38-39; vs. communism, 88, 147-51, 171. *Seealso* Capitalism, regulated; Regulation, economic
Capitalism, regulated, 44-45, 72, 114, 147, 194n11; crisisof, 49-50; and Third World, 50-51. *See also* Capitalism; Regulation, economic
Capital mobility, 51-53, 69-70, 74-75, 79, 153, 176-77; andglobal capital

markets, 52-53; and global factories, 18; and offshore production, 52, 76
Carter, Jimmy, 53, 56
"The Case for Free Trade" (Twentieth Century Fund), 15
Casstevens, Bill, 108, 159
Castañeda, Jorge, 109-10
Caterpillar Company, 108, 158-59
Cavanagh, John, 139-40
Centeno, Humberto, 130
Central American Common Market (CACM), 61
Central Intelligence Agency (CIA), 150
CEOs. *See* Chief Executive Officers
Chief Executive Officers (CEOs), 33
China, 16, 17, 24, 53, 69, 126, 133
CIA. *See* Central Intelligence Agency
CIO. *See* Congress of Industrial Organizations
Citicorp, 30, 70
Civilian Conservation Corps, 43
Civil Works Administration, 43
Clinton, Bill, 15, 27, 30, 70, 74, 90, 132-33, 134, 135
Coalition for Justice in the Maquiladoras, 124-25
Codes of conduct, corporate, 76-77, 123-27, 139-40, 179, 203n37
Cold War, 150-51, 171, 184
Colgate-Palmolive, 31
Columbia, 69
Communications, global, 159-60
Communism, 88, 147-51, 171
Competitiveness, 3, 5, 7, 21, 55; and downsizing, 26; anddownward spiral, 25, 74-75; and job security,

D

International Monetary Fund (IMF): and Bretton Woods System, 45-46; and global ecology, 31; and globalization, 4, 19, 56-58, 60, 62-63, 71, 77; and globalization resistance movement, 85-86, 89, 91-94, 115, 135, 173, 175-76, 177-78; and shock therapy programs, 5, 32, 88, 179; and structural adjustment programs, 5, 22, 27, 30, 78, 164, 179

International NGO Forum, 92-94

International Textile, Garment and Leather Workers' Federation, 111

International trade agreements. *See* General Agreement onTariffs and Trade (GATT); North American Free Trade Agreement (NAFTA); World Trade Organization (WTO)

International Trade Organization, 45

International Trade Secretariats (ITS), 165

International Working Men's Association (1864), 145

Iraq, 75

Italy, 30-31, 161-62, 163

ITS. *See* International Trade Secretariats

J

Jacobi, Peter, 125-26

Japan, 30-31, 68-69, 89, 93, 125, 151, 152, 154; and offshore production, 76; and unemployment, 27, 192n50

Jimenez, Marco, 155

Job security, 22, 23, 44

Johnson Tombigbee Furniture Manufacturing Company, 17, 20, 21

K

Kagarlitsky, Boris, 130-31

Kantor, Micky, 135

Keynes, John Maynard, 42-43, 45

Keynesian policies, 42-43, 44, 152; and capital mobility, 53, 195n10; and labor standards, 122

Khor, Martin, 136-37

Korea, 16, 87, 89-90, 131, 134

Kuwait, 75

L

Labor internationalism: and AFL-CIO reform, 163; andchanging labor interests, 151; in Cold War era, 150-51; communism/capitalism polarity of, 88, 147-51, 171; and cross-border organizing, 156-57; emergence of, 143-145; and global communications, 159-60; and grassroots networking, 163; and ILO conventions ratification, 164; and institutional reform, 164-65; and labor rights, 157, 163; and nationalism, 145-47; new strategies for, 153-54; and North/South dialogue, 164; restructuring, 160-61; andstrike support, 157-59; and worker rights, 162-63; and worker-to-worker exchange, 154-56; in the workplace, 152-53; and workplace agenda, 162; and workplace representation, 161-62. *See also* Globalization resistance

Y

Z

About South End Press

South End Press is a non-profit, collectively run book publisher with more than 200 titles in print. Since our founding in 1977, we have tried to meet the needs of readers who are exploring, or are already committed to, the politics of radical social change.

Our goal is to publish books that encourage ciritical thinking and constructive action on the key political, cultural, social, economic and ecological issues shaping life in the United States and in the world. In this way, we hope to give expression to a wide diversity of democratic social movements and to provide an alternative to the products of corporate publishing.

Through the Institute for Social and Cultural Change, South End Press works with other political media projects—Z magazine; Speak Out, a speakers bureau; and Alternative Radio—to expand access to information and critical analysis.

If you would like a free catalog of South End Press books, please write to us at: South End Press, 7 Brookline Street #1, Cambridge, MA 02139-4146. Visit us on the web at http://www.lbbs.org/sep/sep.htm or email southend@igc.org.

Other South End Press Titles of Interest

Strike! Revised and Updated Edition, South End Press Classics, Volume 1
by Jeremy Brecher

Global Visions: Beyond the New World Order,
edited by Jeremy Brecher, John Brown Childs, and Jill Cutler

Hard-Pressed in the Heartland:
The Hormel Strike and the Future of the Labor Movement,
by Peter Rachleff

About the Authors

Jeremy Brecher is an author and historian whose eight previous books include the labor history classic *Strike!* and the collection *Global Visions: Beyond the New World Order.*

Tim Costello was a truck driver and workplace activist for 20 years. He is currently director of the Massachusetts Campaign on Contingent Work.

Brecher and Costello are the authors of *Common Sense for Hard Times* and the editors of *Building Bridges: The Emerging Coalition of Labor and Community.*

DATE DUE

Printed
in USA

HIGHSMITH #45230